Pat Maher

YORK HAND

GENERAL EDITOR:
Professor A.N. Jeffares
(*University of Stirling*)

D1100642

AN INTRODUCTORY GUIDE TO ENGLISH LITERATURE

Martin Stephen

BA (LEEDS) PH D (SHEFFIELD)
Second Master, Sedbergh School

LONGMAN
YORK PRESS

The illustration of the Globe Playhouse is from
The Globe Restored in Theatre: A Way of Seeing,
by C. Walter Hodges, published by Oxford University Press.
© Oxford University Press

YORK PRESS
Immeuble Esseily, Place Riad Solh, Beirut.

LONGMAN GROUP LIMITED
Longman House,
Burnt Mill,
Harlow,
Essex.

© Librairie du Liban 1984

First published 1984
Reprinted 1985
ISBN 0 582 79278 9

Printed in Hong Kong by
Sheck Wah Tong Printing Press Ltd

Contents

How to use this handbook

This book is designed for students who are starting a course in English literature that will lead to an examination. There is a bewildering variety of books available for students of English literature, ranging from the texts themselves to every conceivable critical aid. This Handbook is designed to save time and money for the average student by putting into one book a basic core of information that can generally be regarded as essential for literature students. It should be read in conjunction with its companion volume, *Preparing for Examinations in English Literature*.

Part 1 deals with essay writing, giving basic advice and information on the most commonly used method of assessment for literature students. The aim here is to cut short the time the student needs to spend on evolving a suitable style and approach in the writing of essays, so that more time can be spent studying and understanding the actual texts.

Part 2 gives a list of definitions of literary terms that are in general use; similar lists of terms peculiar to the conventional divisions of writing (drama, poetry, and the novel) are given later. Thus *irony*, which can be used in all three modes (plays, poems, and novels) is included in Part 2, whereas *apron stage*, which is used solely of drama, is listed under 'Literary Terms' in Part 3: Drama. The aim here is for the student to be able to look up quickly and conveniently any term he comes across which he does not understand, or which causes confusion. Equally, reading through Part 2 gives the student a useful armoury of general terms to use in essays.

There then follow Parts 3, 4 and 5, devoted to drama, poetry and the novel, respectively. Each Part opens with a section called 'Talking Points', which gives an introduction to that particular mode or genre of writing. There are specific problems related to drama, for example, such as the fact that it is performed before a live audience, whereas poems and novels tend to be read by people on their own. Such issues are discussed so the student can find his way in the mode or genre, and know at least a little of what to look out for when he or she starts to read a text. The following section in each of Parts 3, 4 and 5 is a list of literary terms used in that particular mode or genre, and this is followed by a brief history and reading list combined.

The 'History and Reading List' sections run through the leading works in drama, poetry, and prose in chronological order. A minimum of background information is given about each author or group of authors, and some idea of where that author or group fits into the general development of English literature; each author or group is followed by a basic reading list. Again, there are two aims. The first is to give the student an idea of where the author he is studying fits into the general development of literature, and what his or her place is in the history of literature. Secondly, the grouping of authors tells the student who wants to do some background reading which other authors or books might be consulted, and what basic features in them should be considered. The authors included in these groups are not necessarily the most famous in the history of literature, but they are the authors who are set most frequently for examinations. Equally, the books recommended for reading are not always the most famous by their particular author, but they are the easiest ones for a student with little experience of studying literature to understand. These sections can therefore be used as scaled-down literary histories, or as basic guides as to whom and what to read. Finally in each of Parts 3, 4 and 5 there are examples of practical criticism or comment and appreciation exercises for each different mode.

Part 6 is on revision, or the best approach to adopt when coming into the final period of preparation for an examination. Part 7 offers a select reading list, giving publishing details of the various books recommended in the course of the Handbook, with a small number of additional works. The aim here is to let the student find quickly and easily the books he needs – either in libraries or by purchase. It also gives some basic guidance on how to choose the correct critical works.

This Handbook does *not* qualify as a book which tells the student everything he or she needs to know about literature. But it does save the need to purchase five or six other books, at least in the early stages of a course; it provides a hard core of basic information for reference throughout a course; and it tells the student where to find further information.

Part 1

Essays

Writing essays

Any assessment of a literature student's ability will be based to a very large extent on his or her ability to write in essay form on the books studied. The essay is therefore the single most important technique for a student to understand; it is probably the most vital skill that a student of literature has to master. No teacher or book will ever be able to provide you with everything you need to say in an essay; literature studies still demand a personal response from the reader, and a good essay will always contain a certain amount of what a student feels about a book, as well as what he has been told to say. Nevertheless, even though the content of an essay will always depend to a certain extent on personal response, its structure and the conventions that dictate the manner and style in which the essay is written are subject to fairly strict rules.

Starting to think

Every student who starts an 'O' or 'A' level literature course has written essays of one sort or another before. This can create problems. Up to 'O' level, the essays that are set by teachers and examining boards are biased towards language skills rather than literary skills. Most students will be familiar with the various types of language essays: 'argument' essays, where the writer has to argue a firm case for a certain point of view; 'discursive' essays, where a general discussion of a topic of interest is called for; stories; and the 'imaginative' essay, in which a student is asked to give a vivid account of his or her own feelings and emotions. Another type of essay with which the average student will be very familiar is the simple factual account in which a large amount of information is written down in continuous prose. As regards literature, most students will have been asked to write an 'appreciation' of a book – a rather grand word for what is often no more than a bald summary of a book's plot, with a few lines at the end to say whether or not a student liked the book.

The problem is that none of these essays prepare students for what will be asked of them in writing a respectable literature essay; quite reasonably most students try to use the styles and techniques with which they are already familiar to cope with the new task facing them. Rather than use old techniques, it is better to face up to the stark facts right from the beginning: writing literary criticism demands a completely new style, with definite rules and conventions that have to be learned before you can proceed to the interesting part of the course. However important the passenger, he will not reach his destination unless the vehicle he is in is serviceable and in good order; so with an essay, the best ideas possible will come to nothing unless you can develop a way of writing that lets you express them to their best advantage.

So what am I writing?

It is sometimes very difficult to know exactly what is being demanded of you when you start off as a literary critic, and teachers of literature can be infuriatingly persistent in telling a student that his essay is wrong, without telling him how to make it right.

There is endless debate (some of it very heated) about the nature and aims of literary criticism, and any attempt to define it for a student will inevitably arouse howls of protest. However, the task facing a student of literature is much simpler than it is sometimes made out to be. When someone reads a book, it is a wholly personal act; they pick it up, read it, draw their own conclusions, and put it down. No-one can demand that you like the book, or tell you what you must think about it – but when you set out to write an essay on a book, it ceases to be something *personal*, and becomes something *public*. This distinction is vital. You can think what you like when you read a book; when you write an essay on it, you can also think what you like – *but everything you say has to be proved*. Your aim in an essay is *not* to say whether or not you 'like' a book; your aim is to show that you can understand it, and to comment sensibly on it.

In general terms, therefore, your job in an essay is to show you can understand what an author is trying to achieve in writing a work of literature; how well he has succeeded in that task or tasks; and how he has set about trying to achieve his aims. However, the task of writing an essay is usually not as simple as the above might suggest; essay titles tend to ask you to comment on a specific area of a book, and rarely let you write about it in purely general terms. This leads on to the first of the points listed as 'basic mistakes' below.

Basic mistakes

It may seem a little negative to start off with a list of the things not to do when writing an essay, but the most common faults are usually easy to remove, and you cannot get down to the real business of literary studies until you have a purified essay style.

1. *Answer the question*

The single most common cause of failure to write an effective essay is not answering the question. There are two ways in which this can happen, and the most common is to give a plot summary – an account of what happened in the book – instead of writing an answer to the specific question you have been asked. If the essay question is 'Is Hamlet mad?' there is no point at all in just writing down an account of what happens in the scenes where Hamlet shows signs of madness. The person who set the question assumes you have read the play, and that you know what happens in it. He wants you to *interpret* the facts, not merely write them out. After all, Shakespeare tells him what happens in the play better than you are ever likely to do. A comment such as 'Hamlet hurls abuse at his mother' will gain you no marks at all, however true it may be. What you need to say is something along the lines of 'The fact that Hamlet abuses his mother shows that he is under great strain, and has lost control of his emotions, which might suggest that he is mad.' In the first of these sentences, the writer simply tells the reader something that took place in the play; but in the second an interpretation is being put on the bare facts of what happened, and this relates directly to the title of the essay. Faced with a difficult essay subject, the student will sometimes give a long, rambling account of the plot simply because it is the only thing he is certain of, the only thing he feels he knows. The answer is to be very harsh with yourself, and check ruthlessly that every reference to the plot or story is tied in with a statement that is part of a direct answer to the title.

Failure to answer the question can also arise when a student has learnt an essay or set of facts in advance. Teachers sometimes tend to have set ideas, and books – from the shortest Revision Aids to the most advanced works of criticism – all talk about some issues or points of debate, but leave others out. So the student who has found a specimen essay in a book on a certain topic or received a lecture on it from his teacher, quite reasonably feels very pleased with himself when he feels he understands that topic. Frequently that same student will sit down in an examination and write the essay he wants to write and which he feels he knows most about, regardless of whether or not the examiner has actually asked that question. You may have the answer to 'Is Hamlet mad?' at your finger-tips; but woe betide you if you tell the examiner why Hamlet is or is not mad if he is actually asking you something else. However good your essay is, the basic rule is:

No answer to the question = No marks.

Of course, not all essays pose this problem. A character sketch of a certain character in a play or novel, for example, allows you to write down almost everything you know about that character, and as long as what you are writing *is* on that character, it will inevitably be relevant.

The basic rule, therefore, is to make sure you know exactly what it is that you are being asked in an essay, and then to make sure that you only provide information and commentary that are directly relevant.

2. *Clarity and economy*

Another very common mistake is to use a very elaborate or ornate style, in an attempt to make the essay 'sound good'. An example of this style is given below:

> However, when both sides of the argument are considered, it becomes immediately apparent that Hamlet's madness is both a subjective and objective phenomena, and an issue that must wreak havoc with over-simple discussions of the play's structure. What are we to think?

What indeed? This paragraph, or anything even vaguely like it, will send the examiner laughing all the way to the waste paper basket. Its main problem is that *it is not actually saying anything*. It uses long words in a complex structure, and ends on a very fine rhetorical note, but as a way of showing that the writer has understood either the book or the question it is completely useless. The tell-tale sign is the question at the end; good students do not have time to ask questions in their essays, because they are too busy giving the answers. Another tell-tale sign is the use of 'phenomena', the plural, instead of 'phenomenon'. A student who is writing for sound rather than content more often than not uses words in totally the wrong context, or misspells them, a sure sign that it is the 'effect' of the words he is interested in, not their actual meaning. Answer questions in an essay; do not ask them. Never use a long, rambling style and words that you only half understand; always remember that the job of an essay is to convey information as clearly and as economically as possible, and that your mark is decided by the meaning of what you say, not how it sounds.

If you are working towards an examination time will be at a premium when you come to write your essays, and for this reason alone never 'pad out' your essays with meaningless phrases. Quantity is much less important than quality. Never advertise what you are going to do, as, for instance, by saying 'I now propose to look at the points on both sides of this argument'; just go ahead and do it. Try to use 'however' as little as possible, and never use it as a <u>conjunction</u>. Resist the temptation to bluster your way through or ram an argument down an examiner's throat by saying such things as 'It is absolutely clear that . . . ' or 'No-one could deny that . . . '; candidates usually use these phrases to cover up considerable personal doubt as to whether what they are saying is correct or not, and an examiner is convinced by the weight of your evidence, not the loudness of your voice. Never patronise or condescend to the reader, as, for instance, in 'When one has studied the book in great depth, and thought long and hard over it, certain conclusions are inescapable'; this is rather like telling the examiner that you have read the book in more detail than he has, which is a dangerous line to take!

3. *Punctuating the title*
It is one of the basic conventions of criticism that the title of a book or poem is always given special punctuation in an essay, to mark it out from the rest of the text. This is necessary to show the reader when you are referring to a complete book; for example, it is essential that a reader should know if you mean *Hamlet* the play, or Hamlet the character within the play, even though the rule applies to books with titles that are less liable to cause confusion.

The rules are very simple. To be absolutely correct you should underline the title of a book, and place inverted commas round the title of a poem. Never do both. The title is always written out in full: *Much Ado About Nothing* is correct, whilst *Much Ado* is not. Start each word of the title with a capital letter, unless the title page of the book prints it differently, as *The War of the Worlds*; in any event, check the correct punctuation from the title page, and learn it. This is one of the things that you can teach yourself very early on in your course, so that it quickly becomes instinctive.

4. *Quotations*
There are three basic mistakes easily made when introducing quotations into an essay: misquoting, quoting at too great length, and turning poetry into prose. As an aside, it is worth learning the difference between 'quote' and 'quotation'. 'Quote' is a verb, and so you can never allow yourself to talk about 'a quote'; you need the noun form, which is 'quotation'. You do not have 'quotes' in an essay – you have 'quotations'. It is a point which some traditional examiners react to very strongly.

It is essential that you quote accurately, down to the last comma and capital letter, even if it seems to you that the writer has made a mistake. If you write out a quotation that does contain a grammatical mistake, you can always write '(sic)' – the Latin for 'thus' – after it, which is the conventional way of showing that it was the original writer's mistake, rather than your own. Examiners do check quotations for accuracy, and a student who quotes incorrectly is like a lawyer who gives false evidence: doubt is thrown on the accuracy of *anything* he says. On a more personal level, most authors take it as a personal insult to have their work misquoted; if a man's reputation is going to be based on what he wrote, it is only fair to make sure you write down exactly what he said.

The use of quotations is vital in an essay, as a major source of evidence for whatever viewpoint you are adopting, but it can be overdone. Long quotations break up the flow of an essay, and there is always the risk that an essay will contain more material written by the original author than by the candidate. There is no virtue in your knowing vast chunks of a book, play, or poem off by heart; it is the relevance of what you quote to what you are trying to prove or state that gains the marks, and showing off how many lines you have learnt loses more marks than it gains.

If a quotation is two lines or less in the original text, it can be 'run on' in your essay without starting a new line. All that is needed is a comma before the quotation, and the quotation marked off with inverted commas, as in the following:

> Wells's style is simple and unadorned. It can also be careless, as when he writes, 'The house was never clean nor tidy', where 'or' should be used in place of 'nor'.

If it is poetry that you are quoting, you can still run on a quotation of two lines or less, but the end of one line and the start of another must be marked by a diagonal line:

> Othello's anger is clearly heard in the lines, 'Now, by heaven,/My blood begins my safer guides to rule'.

Where a quotation occupies more than two lines in the original text, it should be preceded by a comma, started on a new line, and indented (given an extra left-hand margin). Inverted commas are not strictly essential here, but can be useful for complete clarity:

> Othello's anger is clearly heard in the lines,
>
> > 'Now by heaven,
> > My blood begins my safer guides to rule,
> > And passion, having my best judgement collied,
> > Assays to lead the way.'
>
> This speech marks the start of Othello's breakdown.

If something is written as poetry, it is essential that you should quote it as poetry, keeping to the original line arrangements. Poetry is written in lines, and if you run the lines on into each other you are converting poetry into prose, and showing the examiner that you cannot tell the difference between them. It does not suggest you are a very sensitive critic if you cannot spot when something is written as poetry . . . .

5. *Errors of taste*
Never try to win your way to the examiner's heart by flattering the author. Comments such as:

> It is at this moment that the sheer brilliance of Shakespeare's art overwhelms the reader, as the magic of his mighty verse line proves once again that he is the greatest playwright of all time.

All this is very well, but an examiner is likely to view it with a sceptical eye.

Avoid using slang or casual phrases in your essay. A list of common slang terms would fill a whole book, and these terms alter with fashion and the times, but some of the words and phrases to be avoided are: 'brilliant'; 'terrific'; 'fabulous'; 'mind-blowing'; 'nice'; 'nasty'; 'naughty'; 'clever'; 'earth-shattering'; 'hugely'; 'fantastic'; and 'boring'. *Never* describe a work of literature, or a part of it, as being 'boring'; it only suggests the type of candidate you are.

Never be flippant in an essay. The aim of an essay is to convey a certain point of view or display an understanding of a book; it is not to make an examiner laugh, and in any event most attempts at humour in an essay fall flat. The candidate who wrote

> The moment when Macbeth peers into the witches' cauldron is of great dramatic significance and tension – unless, of course, his beard falls off in the steam and goes in with the witches' brew!

might well raise a laugh, but was doing so in the wrong place and at the wrong time.

Never start an essay with, 'I propose to look at both sides of this case, and then to come to a conclusion' (it is obvious that is what you will be doing, and it does not need stating); never end an essay with, 'This is a very difficult question, and having looked at all the relevant issues, I find it impossible to come to a conclusion' (there would be no point in an essay that was not difficult, and it is your job to come to a conclusion).

6. *Tenses*

Do not write your essay in the past tense. The events in a book, play, or poem happen anew every time the book is read. They have happened (past tense) in the past when anyone has read the book or seen the play acted; they are happening now (present tense), whenever someone reads or sees the work; they will happen (future tense) in the future, when the same thing happens again. Thus if you say, 'Macbeth was lured by the witches and Lady Macbeth into the murder of Duncan' you are implying it will never happen again. You could, of course, write, 'Macbeth was, is, and will be lured ... ', but the simplest way, and the best compromise, is to use the present tense: 'Macbeth is lured ... '.

Positive points

---

1. *Planning*

This is probably the most over-used word in any classroom where literature is being taught. Many students react to the pressure placed on them to plan essays by ignoring it, or if they have to produce a plan with an essay, writing the plan after they have written the essay.

The standard arguments for not planning an essay are that it takes too much time, and that the student writes a better essay without a plan. The answer to the first complaint is that planning an essay does take a great deal of time, particularly at the start. That is also why it is essential to start planning essays right at the beginning of a course in literary studies. In an examination, a plan will need to be done in five minutes, and it takes a great deal of practice to bring the amount of time needed down to this figure. The answer to the second complaint is that the student does not write a better essay when it is unplanned. It may be fine for a Romantic poet to compose his verses in a sudden flash of inspiration, but a literature student has to get down a great deal of information at the right time and in the right place, and is more like someone drawing up a railway timetable than a creative author; it is not difficult to foresee what would happen if railway timetables were written down spontaneously and without advance planning, and disaster of a different sort faces the student who fails to plan his essays.

What unfortunately happens is that someone who is used to writing without a plan tends to write rather bad essays for the first two or three times that he or she tries to plan. The discipline of planning cramps their old, spur-of-the-moment style, and it takes some time for a new style to emerge. The trick is to keep going. It is worth it; anyone who sits down in an examination without a developed planning technique is like someone who jumps into the sea wearing lead boots and without a life jacket; the person will sink without trace, and so will the essay.

A number of things happen when a student first sets his eyes on an essay title. Once he has understood what the title is asking (not always so easy in recent times, with examiners seemingly going for more and more long-winded titles), some ideas are bound to come into his head as to what he might write, always assuming he has done a reasonable amount of work on the text. These ideas do not emerge in any rational or logical order. Some will be useful, some trivial, some wrong, and some will need further thought. The first thing to do is to write down all these ideas as they come into your head, each idea or thought on a different line. If you are not writing under examination conditions, make sure you have looked through the text and any notes you might have made on the text, so that *every* idea you might use in the essay goes down on the paper. Use the briefest of notes for this – the plan is for your use only, and so there is no need to write in complete sentences, or even to be neat.

What you are looking at on that sheet of paper is a plan of what you would have written if you were not prepared to do a proper plan. Some students write down all their preliminary ideas, in the order that they happen to come into their heads, and then just write out what they have written, with no attempt to alter or change it; if this is all that is done, there is no point in writing down the details in the first place. It is the second stage in planning that is the crucial one, what takes place after you have jotted down your rough ideas.

When all the information has been written down, you should decide what your viewpoint will be in the essay. Very often you will have reached a conclusion about the title when you first read it, but it is always wise to check this idea when you have written down in plan form as much of the relevant information as possible. An instinctive, spur-of-the-moment decision can sometimes be wrong, and if it is, the student finds himself arguing fiercely for one point of view, when all his information points the other way.

Look at what you have jotted down, and go through it first for material that no longer seems relevant; there is usually quite a lot of information that seemed good in the first flush of enthusiasm for an essay, but which seems rather less attractive when looked at a second time. Then try to shape your material into four or five paragraphs, each with something definite to say about the title. The exact number of paragraphs will vary with the essay, and the level at which it is being examined, but the majority of essays have not less than three paragraphs, and not more than six. Once you have sorted out what will be in your paragraphs, try to write a 'topic' or 'theme' sentence for each one. The aim of this sentence is to state clearly and directly what the main statement of the paragraph will be. This is perhaps the most difficult technique of all to grasp, but it is essential. A large number of students prefer to build up to a conclusion, only saying what their paragraph is about right at the end, after they have presented their information and evidence. In effect a topic sentence is a conclusion, or summary of your views, but it comes at the start of the paragraph, not at the end. There are a number of reasons why this is such a helpful and necessary technique. Firstly, it allows the student to see if his paragraph *has* a point to it; if you cannot write a topic sentence for your paragraph, it usually means that your paragraph is not actually saying anything, and should be cut out. Secondly, if the topic sentence is an accurate summary of the views expressed in the following paragraph, it is a relatively easy task to look at it and ask if it also forms a direct answer to the essay title. Again, if this is not the case, then the paragraph is irrelevant, and should be deleted. Most important of all, the examiner is given first of all a statement of what you are trying to say. With this in mind, clearly and concisely stated, he can then judge if your evidence and argument are satisfactory, whereas if he is presented with the information and evidence first, he has to wait until the end of the paragraph to see if it is relevant. With the topic sentence as the first words of a paragraph, the main point the writer is trying to make can be punched home to the reader, before it is submerged in a mass of evidence or elaboration.

The next stage is to organise the paragraphs into some order that will help the view expressed in the essay, make the essay easy to read and follow, and give the ideas expressed their best possible chance of doing their job. Try not to jump from one line or argument to another, but let the paragraphs follow on smoothly from each other, building up to the conclusion. Then write an introduction and conclusion, find some quotations to illustrate your points – and write the essay! With the plan in front of you, extra points that come to mind when you are writing can be squeezed into the plan where they will do most good, instead of being written down immediately, regardless of whether or not it is the right time, in order not to forget them.

Planning to this level of complexity is a long and often tedious business. It is, of course, far too long to be of any great usefulness in an examination, but a student who has learnt to plan an essay in this way will not need to go through the full process outlined above. The point about the process is that after a few months the student becomes accustomed to thinking more logically and clearly, and in paragraphs, and as a result a plan can be jotted down, with correct paragraphing and all the other features of a longer plan, in five or six minutes. The first noting down of rough ideas and the final production of a neat and logical plan can be done at the same time – but it takes practice and skill, both of which can only be gained by use of the full-length planning technique given here.

2. *Introductions*

Most essays require an Introduction, that is a preliminary paragraph that comes before the main discussion of the topic in question. An Introduction might be a brief history of an author and his work, but this should be avoided if it runs the risk of being irrelevant. If the essay title asks for discussion of a specific topic, the Introduction could be used to suggest the other main areas of interest in the appropriate text, to show the examiner that the candidate is aware of other issues than the one focussed on in the title. An Introduction can also 'place' a work by an author in the context of his other writings, showing how it relates to other works by the same author, or it can do the same thing as regards contemporary work – work that was being written at the same time. An Introduction can also discuss the work in general, and suggest how the topic covered by the essay fits in with other areas for discussion in the book. The main aim of an Introduction is to give the examiner or reader a gentle lead-in to the essay, and to give necessary or useful background information to the topic under discussion. An Introduction should be short: six or seven lines of normal handwriting might well be sufficient, while more than ten or twelve lines may well start to be too long and undermine the effectiveness of the opening statement.

3. *Conclusions*

Every essay should have a conclusion, the aim of which is to present the examiner or reader with a basic summary of the points made in the essay. It forms an essential part of any essay, and the student must ensure that he always leaves the reader with a firm and clear summary of what has been said in the essay. It is sometimes advised that the conclusion should raise or bring in a new point, to end the essay on a high note. This is usually a very bad idea. If the new idea is worth very much it should have been raised in the main body of the essay; if it is not, then it is probably not worth using.

4. *Critics*

It is essential that the student develops an effective essay style as early as possible in his course of study. The points made above are of general necessity; to gain some idea of how a good essay is written, look at the specimen answers in a relevant *York Notes*, and see how the author presents his ideas. It is also worth striking a cautious note about the use of critics and other books to help in the writing of an essay. Anything that helps you to think and enlarges your knowledge of a book is a good thing, but anything that stops you thinking, and acts as a substitute for your own thoughts, is a very bad thing indeed. Do not quote directly from critics in your essay: apart from any other factors, you will never be able to remember their exact words in an examination. Instead, read through a critical text and make brief notes when anything is written that actually helps you to understand the book you are studying. Put the ideas *in your own words*; the job of doing this will in itself force you to check what has been written, and see whether or not you do really understand it. You might well find yourself adding to the critic's ideas a few of your own. Always make notes on anything you read, otherwise you will forget it within a week. Finally, never assume that what you read is of necessity correct. Critics make mistakes just as much as anyone else, and very often what you are reading will be an *opinion*, not a fact; as an opinion, it may be interesting, but it can never be taken as a final answer. An essay should never consist of a match between two or more critics, in which the student tries to referee a game between two other people's points of view. The phrases such as 'Critics have stated . . . ' or 'One group of critics believe . . ..' suggest that the student has no views of his own. An examination mark given to an essay that simply contains the views of published critics is a mark given to the critics, not the student.

5. *Presentation*

Some people are neat, some are not, but there is no need to lose marks or give a bad impression by presenting an essay that is scruffy and looks as if it were written by somebody disorganised and uncaring. Write out the title of the essay in full at the top of the page; apart from helping the examiner or reader, it gives you a few extra moments to think about the title, and a surprising number of students realise they have misunderstood what the title is asking for when they come to write it out. Underline the whole title with a ruler, and leave a clear line between the title and the start of your essay. Try to write with a fountain pen. It is more awkward, but it is actually less likely to blot than a ball point, and the nib skids across the page much less, the result usually being that essays written with a fountain pen are more legible. Do not use different coloured inks for quotations, or do anything other than the suggestions given earlier in this chapter for the presentation of quotations. Never write headings for separate paragraphs, unless the question specifically asks you to split up your answer into a number of sub-headings. Cross out with a single line through the incorrect word or phrase, not with a scrawling mass of lines that becomes a focal point for the whole page. Cross out rather than use the fluids which are now on the market, usually designed for typescript; these fluids rarely take kindly to being written, as distinct from typed, over, and the process of applying the fluid and then waiting for it to dry takes far too long.

6. *General points*

No two essays are alike. They differ because the titles are different, the books are different, and the demands placed on the student are different, from the person writing in the peace and quiet of his own home to the person with a mere half hour in which to display all he knows about a certain book or author. Despite these differences, good essays do have many things in common. They are neat, well planned, and written in a clear, straightforward style. They are strictly relevant to the question being asked, and never simply an account of everything the student knows about a given topic or book. Finally, a good essay is convincing, not only because what it contains is based on a student's own observations and feelings, but because that student has taken a firm grip on the principles of evidence and is able to prove the points made. It is not enough for the writer to feel that he is right; he has to give good reasons why others should share his opinion. It is not enough for the student to state what he feels and thinks; he has to prove, as far as he is able, that his viewpoint is a valid one.

One example of a case in which the laws of evidence come firmly into focus is that of a student with deeply-held religious convictions. He might very well find himself having to write an essay on a novel or play which seems to deny the validity of religion, and even pours scorn on it. The student cannot condemn this work in his essay simply because it goes against what he believes to be right. He must swallow his own hostility, at least until he has found out exactly what the author is trying to say. If he is going to condemn the book in question it cannot be done solely on the grounds that the author has written a book that the student does not agree with; the student's view has to be shown to have validity for the average reader (a convenient invention, even if such a creature rarely exists in practice), whose views on religion might be totally different. It is not good criticism to condemn a book for holding one particular viewpoint; it is perfectly valid to condemn an author for having failed to express his views convincingly, where, for example, his case rests on characters who are unconvincingly or badly portrayed, or on a plot which can be shown to have inaccuracies in it. This can be a fine distinction, and a book such as this Handbook cannot hope to go into this area of personal preferences in any depth, but can merely warn about some of the dangers that face the unsuspecting student. It used to be said that politics and religion were topics to be avoided at dinner parties, as being liable to provoke argument and upset; there is no such restriction on the student writing a literary essay, but he might well be advised to pause before commenting on an author's treatment of these areas, just to check that he is not condemning an author for failing to write what he, the student, would have written had he been in a position to write the novel.

The final point as regards evidence is to ask if there is a passage or incident from the text to prove every point that has been made in an essay. If the answer is no, that point needs careful examination to see if it is valid. There is no point in saying, 'Hamlet's madness is an act, a defensive gesture by Hamlet to avert suspicion from his real motives' unless you can find a line or incident to back up the point (there is one, incidentally: Hamlet says as much to Horatio early on in the play).

The different types of essay

All the previous discussion has concentrated on the essay as a general issue, but of course there are several different types of essay that can be set, and it is sometimes a help to 'place' or categorise an essay by type, in order to understand more clearly what one is being asked.

1. The factual account
Occasionally you will be asked to write a straightforward account of what happens in a scene or episode. This type of question is only occasionally set, and then never in advanced level examination papers. Most often the examiner will choose a scene of considerable complexity, with a large number of characters or incidents, and the aim of the question is simply to test factual knowledge. The only thing to remember is to time this essay very carefully, selecting only the crucial incidents and events; occasionally students pack in so many facts that they find their time runs out when they are only half way through the scene.

2. *The character sketch*

This can be asked of plays, novels, or even certain narrative poems, and its object is to find out if a student has understood what the main elements are in the portrait of one or more characters, and how those elements or features have been created by the author. You should distinguish between the essay which asks you to give an account of a character, and the essay which questions you on specific aspects of a character. Thus the essay 'What are the main elements of Hamlet's character' is very different from 'Is Hamlet a "sweet prince" or an "arrant knave"?' The first essay is a general description, the second is a specific question which must be answered. One of the most common mistakes in answering essays on character is to give an account of the character's actions when what is actually required is a commentary on certain aspects of a character. Normally, a straightforward character sketch is only asked of minor or lesser characters, whilst on major character essays tend to be on one aspect of a character, and tend also to be a specific question requiring a specific answer. A general rule is never to write down everything you know about a character unless you are specifically told to do just that. For general character sketches, always base each paragraph round a feature of the character.

3. *Opposed viewpoints*

One of the most common types of essay is that which presents the student with two different, opposed viewpoints. One such title has already been mentioned – 'Is Hamlet a "sweet prince" or an "arrant knave"?' Here you need to know what your answer is before you start to write the essay. Without this safeguard you will tend either to write in the most general terms about Hamlet, and not answer the question, or argue both sides of the argument with equal strength, and leave the issue hanging in the balance at the end.

Always remember that a convincing exposition of one viewpoint looks at the arguments on the other side of the question. Thus if you happen to think that Hamlet is a 'sweet prince', to convince an examiner that this is a valid and logical view you must look at the reasons why he might be seen as an 'arrant knave', and show why these reasons are outweighed by other ones. Leave the examiner with the arguments for the view you are supporting as the last section in the essay, and look at opposing viewpoints earlier on. Do not assume that you have to prove that these opposing viewpoints are wrong; all you have to do is show that the other viewpoints, and the evidence for them, are more convincing. Thus there is no doubt that Hamlet kills Polonius and Laertes, and treats Ophelia very badly; these are facts which cannot be denied, and they tend to support the view of him as an arrant knave. It could, however, also be argued that he kills Polonius by accident, and it is Polonius's fault that he is killed; that Laertes is trying to kill Hamlet, so Hamlet's murdering Laertes is self-defence; and that Ophelia betrays Hamlet, and so deserves all she gets. It is possible to explain away these apparent blemishes on Hamlet's character. If one believes that Gertrude (Hamlet's mother) is an innocent character, then his treatment of her is that of an 'arrant knave', and cannot really be excused, but the existence of one fact that suggests he is an 'arrant knave' does not prove the idea – it all depends on how many facts there are on the other side of the argument. If you know which side you are arguing on from the start of the essay it will very often fall into place as a logical exposition of a point of view; if you do not know, it will ramble, and contradict itself.

4. *Discussion*

When an essay title says 'discuss', it does not mean 'illustrate'. A large number of students, when faced with a quotation and essay title such as ' "The main theme of *Hamlet* is revenge." Discuss.' assume that they have to illustrate the truth of this statement, rather than argue it as something which is merely a point of view. The essay which asks the student to discuss an issue is perhaps the most common one there is, and what the word really means is 'explore' or even 'analyse the truth of' the statements given. *There is no need always to agree with the statement made in the title of an essay*; your job is to discuss it and reach a conclusion on it, not to agree with it of necessity. In the above title, the essay must centre on the issue of revenge, but if the student feels that revenge is not the main theme of the play – and even if he does – he will have to look at other themes. To say that revenge is important in the play does not prove it is the *most* important theme, and this issue can only be decided by examining other possible contenders for the title of 'most important theme'.

Discussion means working round a title or topic, analysing its implications and wider issues. As always, the essay must lead to a conclusion, firmly stated and argued.

5. *Dramatic significance and contribution*

If your set text is a play you may be asked to comment on the dramatic significance of a scene or character; if it is a novel you may be asked what contribution is made to the book by a certain episode or character. This type of essay is, in other words, asking you to illustrate the manner in which an episode or character contributes to the wider effect of the book.

The first stage here is to list all that the scene or episode achieves: does it contribute to the themes of the book; the plot; the characterisation? (If it is a character that is under discussion, the questions are identical.) When you have a list, separate it into the various headings, starting with the features in the scene or episode, and building up to the general significance. For example, the dramatic significance of the first scene in

Hamlet is that it creates an atmosphere of tension, uncertainty, and corruption which is amplified and played on in the rest of the play; it is also highly 'dramatic', that is, it grips the audience's imagination with its talk of ghosts and deaths, thus gaining their attention at the start of the play when the author needs to make the maximum impact. The first chapter of Charles Dickens's novel *Bleak House* talks at length about a London fog. The contribution this makes is again to create an atmosphere that relates to the rest of the novel, in this instance one of blindness and confusion, and to start a line of imagery in the novel connected with water. Always start with what the scene or episode does, and move on to its wider contribution to the book as a whole. An essay based on a specific scene or episode may lead on to wider issues, but it must always start with the part of the text detailed by the title.

6. *Final points*
Unlike many other academic subjects, literature studies do not always present the student with a question to which there is a right or a wrong answer. Literature is about personal perception and understanding, about communication, about imagination. It is possible to answer an essay in one of a number of ways, each of which could be right, depending on the skill with which the student presents his viewpoint. Always remember that having a point of view – even if it is wrong – is worth a great deal to the literature student.

Part 2

Literary terms in general use

LITERATURE HAS ITS OWN SPECIAL LANGUAGE, as does any academic subject, and the student needs to know his way round the various literary terms as they are used by critics, and as he will have to use them himself. The list in this chapter consists of terms that are used for all the three types of writing – drama, poetry, and prose. Terms used in connection with one type of writing only are dealt with separately in the section devoted to that type.

Words in small capital letters in the definitions are to be found as headwords, with their own definitions, elsewhere in this list. If you are not sure of the meaning of these words, look them up in their separate entries, which are placed in alphabetical order.

The dates of the authors in the various lists of literary terms in this Handbook are given only the first time the authors are mentioned.

allegory: a story or narrative, usually of some length, which carries a second meaning, as well as that of its surface story; an allegory is usually a method of telling one story whilst seeming to tell another. An allegory can be prose, poetry, or drama. Probably the most famous prose allegory is *The Pilgrim's Progress* by John Bunyan (1628–88), first published as a whole in 1684. As with many allegories, this has characters who are incarnations of abstract ideas, and personifications of human virtues, vices and characteristics such as Mr Worldly-Wise, Giant Despair, Hopeful, Lechery, Pride, and Christian, the pilgrim. The most famous poetic allegory is probably *The Faerie Queen* (1596) by Edmund Spenser (?1552–99). The Queen of the title is Spenser's own Queen Elizabeth I of England, and the six books of the poem are allegories of the Anglican Church, Temperance, Chastity, Friendship, Justice, and Courtesy, each abstract virtue being personified (see PERSONIFICATION). One of the most famous allegories in play form is *Everyman* (?1500), the theme of which is the summoning of Everyman by Death; of all his friends, only Good Deeds will follow Everyman, the others (Fellowship, Kindred, Goods, Knowledge, Beauty, Strength, and so on) refusing to make this sacrifice. Though not always seen as an allegory, the novel *Animal Farm* (1945) by George Orwell (1903–50) tells the story of the rise of Communism in Russia, and the Russian Revolution, with animals representing the people involved, and the different countries being represented by farms. This novel is SATIRE, but satire based on a strong allegorical structure.

ambiguity: in the original meaning of the word, ambiguity refers to a word or phrase the meaning of which is unclear, often through the fault or weakness of the author. However, a modern view sees ambiguity as a recognised and valuable literary technique, and one by which an author can suggest many layers or levels of meaning, thus enriching his book. This type of ambiguity is sometimes referred to as *multiple meanings*, *fruitful* or *wilful* ambiguity. Used in this manner ambiguity can allow an author to present several contradictory incidents or episodes, so as to reveal the full complexity of a situation. It was the critic William Empson (*b*.1906) who focussed attention on this technique in his book *Seven Types of Ambiguity* (1947), and showed how many striking effects come from conscious or unconscious double meanings; the student who wishes to know more should seek out one of the numerous modern editions of this book. A confusing element for the student can come from the link between ambiguity and IRONY. As a basic guide, a passage is ambiguous where it has no clear meaning, and ironical where it has several. Ambiguity normally illustrates a sense of uncertainty, irony the opposite.

anachronism: a historically inaccurate episode or event. The clock chiming in *Julius Caesar* (1599) by William Shakespeare (1564–1616) is an anachronism: mechanical clocks had not been invented in Roman times, in which the play is supposedly set.

bathos: a sudden and unintentional descent into the ludicrous and ridiculous, usually where the author is intending to achieve a noble or moving effect. This must be differentiated from anti-climax, where for comic effect an author creates this sudden drop from seriousness to comedy.

burlesque: another aspect of ridicule. A burlesque is a work that sets out to ridicule a style or type of writing, either by writing in a trivial manner about a serious subject, or by writing in a serious manner about a trivial subject. There are comparatively few examples of pure burlesque (one example is *Tom Thumb* (1730) by Henry Fielding (1707–54)), if only because burlesque is closely related to a number of other genres, notably PARODY and MOCK HEROIC. A basic definition is that burlesque ridicules a whole style or attitude in literature; parody ridicules a particular book or work. Thus Fielding's *Tom Thumb* is burlesque because it ridicules a whole style of inflated, tragic writing that was current in Fielding's day, and found in any number of plays. Another book by Fielding, *Shamela* (1741), is closer to parody, even though it uses many of the same techniques as *Tom Thumb*, at least as regards comedy, because it ridicules one particular book, *Pamela* (1740) by Samuel Richardson (1689–1761).

caricature: a character whose personality centres on a small number of exaggerated features; characterisation by means of a very small number of features. Caricature characters often have 'label' names which describe their character. Examples are M'Choakumchild, the repressive schoolmaster in *Hard Times* (1854) by Charles Dickens (1812–70), or Sir Tunbelly Clumsy in *The Relapse* (1696), a play by Sir John Vanbrugh (1664–1726). See also FLAT AND ROUND CHARACTERS.

cliché: any phrase, METAPHOR or SIMILE, or even any idea, that has been used so often, and is so well worn, that it has lost its original inventiveness or appeal.

flat and round characters: terms used to describe two extremes of characterisation, most commonly in the novel, but also useful for drama criticism. A flat character is one who can be summed up very briefly, perhaps even in one sentence; he or she is a 'type', a CARICATURE, or character with little depth or complexity. A flat character is predictable, and always behaves or talks in the same way. A round character is more complex, can surprise the reader with his or her actions, and very often changes or grows in the course of the book. As a general rule flat characters are simple, round characters are complex; it is often true that flat characters are used for comic effect, whilst round characters are used for the more serious or tragic roles. Most novelists combine both types of character in their novels. In *Great Expectations* (1861) by Charles Dickens, the central character, Pip, is a round character; there are also numerous flat characters, such as Wopsle, the failed tragedian, and Trabb's Boy, an assistant to a shopkeeper who has the one single feature of being cheeky and impertinent. For more information, consult *Aspects of the Novel* by E. M. Forster (see Part 7: Select Reading List).

genre: (*French*, type, kind). This term is used in literary criticism to indicate the mode or category of writing to which a work belongs. Poetry, drama and the novel are all *genres.*

humours: the four humours were originally four fluids thought to exist in the human body, and which by their different proportions dictated both a person's personality and his health. References to this belief can be found in most medieval and some Shakespearian works, and any reference to humours in a work up to the middle of the seventeenth century can be taken to have this meaning, in one of two varieties. Earlier references refer to the basic fluids and the features they were meant to give to people. Thus a person with an excess of the humour *blood* in him was called *sanguine*, and was pleasure-loving, amorous, kind, and jovially good-natured; the Franklin in *The Canterbury Tales* (?1387) by Geoffrey Chaucer (?1345–1400) is just such a person. Someone with an excess of *phlegm* in them was described as *phlegmatic*, and was dull, cowardly, unresponsive, dour, and unexciting. An excess of *yellow bile* led a person to be *choleric*, and obstinate, vengeful, impatient, intolerant, angry, and quick to rise to temper. An excess of *black bile* produced a *melancholic* personality: moody, brooding, sharp-tongued, liable to sudden changes of mood, someone lost in thought and contemplation. The poet John Donne (?1571–1631) was supposed to be highly melancholic.

One element in the theory of humours was that a person's personality could be linked to one feature, or at least a recognisable group of features, and another was that physical appearance and personality are linked. Therefore by the start of the seventeenth century the idea had developed from its original medieval base into the 'comedy of humours'. In the comedy of humours people's behaviour was often determined by one trait or humour, and the play *Every Man In His Humour* (1598) by Ben Jonson (1572–1637) is the strongest single example of this type of writing and theory of personality, where almost every character is dominated by a single trait or humour. In a play such as this the word 'humour' means a dominant feature of personality or physique; in its earlier form the word meant simply one of the four humours which medieval science thought existed with the body. The latter usage has obvious links with CARICATURE and FLAT CHARACTERS. In medieval science the four humours were closely linked to the four elements – earth, air, fire, and water – from which all matter on earth was created.

hyperbole: deliberate exaggeration on the part of an author, in order to emphasise a point. The Metaphysical poets (see p. 79) make frequent use of hyperbole, as do a number of other major authors at various times. John Keats (1795–1821) uses hyperbole in his 'Ode to a Nightingale':

> Where but to think is to be full of sorrow
>   And leaden-eyed despairs;
> Where Beauty cannot keep her lustrous eyes,
>   Or new Love pine at them beyond tomorrow.

imagery: this word is used to mean a great many things by a great many critics nowadays, and the only method for the bemused student to adopt is to go for the simplest definition. In its most basic form, imagery is descriptive language; an image itself can be either a single word or a phrase, imagery is simply the plural form used to denote more than one image. It is most often thought of as visual pictures, but an image can also refer to and describe any of the four other senses (taste, touch, hearing, smell). More often than not, an image is written in the form of a SIMILE or METAPHOR. Modern criticism has attached great importance to imagery, partly because an analysis of an author's images can give an insight into his imaginative vision, the way he sees a whole text or book in his head; the more specific the atmosphere or 'feel' that an author wishes to convey, the more his or her imagery will 'cluster' round certain topics or ideas. Robert Burns's (1759–96) 'My love is like a red, red rose' is a simple and effective image, as is Shakespeare's Hamlet battling against 'the slings and arrows of outrageous fortune'. Though not a simile or metaphor, there is a supremely powerful image at the heart of 'The Tyger', a poem by William Blake (1757–1827):

Tyger! Tyger! burning bright
In the forests of the night,
What immortal hand or eye
Could frame thy fearful symmetry?

It takes time and knowledge to become clear about the exact nature of imagery. The answer, as with IRONY is to take the simple way – in this case, to view an image as any descriptive language, and most commonly as a simile or metaphor – and leave the complexities until later on.

irony: irony is a word or phrase that says one thing and means another. In other words, irony occurs when a word or phrase has one surface meaning, and another, contradictory meaning beneath this surface. Irony depends for its success on the reader perceiving the real or inner meaning, rather than the apparent surface meaning. Irony should not be confused with sarcasm, which is purely oral and a very crude form of spoken irony. There are a number of different types of irony. *Verbal* or *rhetorical irony* occurs when a character says something which is the exact opposite of what he or she actually feels. When Hamlet says he is 'but mad north-northwest' he means he is not mad at all. *Socratic irony* occurs when a character pretends to adopt his opponents' views, but in doing so reveals their flaws and weaknesses so as to render them ridiculous. *Dramatic irony* occurs when a character on stage speaks lines which have another meaning to the audience, unknown to the character on stage. One of the best-known examples of this is in Shakespeare's tragedy *Macbeth* (1605–6), when Duncan the King of Scotland enters Macbeth's castle and remarks 'This castle hath a fine and pleasant seat'. The audience have just seen Lady Macbeth swear to kill Duncan that very night in the castle, so there is a huge and horrific irony in Duncan's praise of it which is totally lost on Duncan himself.

There are a number of other types of irony which are sometimes defined, but the word *irony* on its own, and *dramatic irony*, are usually the only two terms the student needs to be familiar with. A slightly confusing factor is the use made of the word irony by some relatively modern critics to suggest any work of literature that is complicated and obscure, suggesting the many 'ironies' of life, where things do not always go according to plan or according to logic. Any complex vision of life can therefore sometimes be described as ironic; however, as a usage it is not universal, and probably creates more confusion than it solves.

The novelist Jane Austen (1775–1817) is a master of irony. So also is the novelist Henry Fielding. The use of irony in a passage from his *Tom Jones* (1749) is discussed in full on pp. 133–5.

malapropism: a type of verbal humour where a speaker substitutes for the correct word one with a similar sound but wholly different meaning. The term derives from Mrs Malaprop, a character in the play *The Rivals* (1775) by Richard Brinsley Sheridan (1751–1816). Dogberry in Shakespeare's *Much Ado About Nothing* (?1589) is addicted to the use of malapropisms, as in ' . . . thou wilt be condemned into everlasting redemption for this'.

metaphor: a comparison between two objects for the purpose of describing one of them; a metaphor states that the one object is the other. Thus the opening line of John Keats's 'Ode on a Grecian Urn' – 'Thou still unravish'd bride of quietness' – is a metaphor. The urn or vase that Keats is referring to is not an 'unravished bride', but the comparison between these two dissimilar objects suggests that the urn has all the qualities of the bride, notably beauty, stillness, and innocence. For this to be a *simile* the words 'like' or 'as' would have to have been used. A *mixed metaphor* occurs when two metaphors are used of the same object, and the two metaphors are hugely different or opposed, as in 'His mind was a hollow shell, with the consistency and intelligence of concrete'.

mock heroic: the style which uses the grand, elevated, and noble style of the epic poem (see p. 77) to deal with a trivial and base subject, the result being a comic effect. The best-known example of this style of writing is Alexander Pope's (1688–1744) *The Rape of the Lock* (1714).

muses: originally in Greek mythology there were nine muses, each presiding over a particular area; areas included epic poetry, love poetry, lyric poetry, tragedy, songs, and comedy. These Muses came to be identified with literature and the arts in general, and from Shakespeare onward the Muses (or a single Muse) are seen as inspirations to poetry and the writing of great literature. For the ordinary student of literature one of the most famous invocations of the Muses is likely to be in Shakespeare's *Henry V* (1599), where Chorus opens the play with the lines 'O! for a Muse of fire, that would ascend/The brightest heaven of invention . . .'

myth: a myth is an anonymous story which tells of often mysterious and strange events far back in history. *Mythology* is a collection of such stories. Myths often deal with elemental situations such as the creation of the world or the actions of gods, and are associated with primitive societies. One feature of myths is that they seem to retain their power and attraction over thousands of years of history, either because they deal with stories and settings that are basic to human life, or because they seem to appeal to some basic instinct in humans which has little to do with a particular era or civilisation. Many authors have created mythologies of their own, such as the poet William Blake, and, in more recent times, the poet Robert Graves (b.1895). Other modern authors have used ancient myths extensively in the preparation of their own works. *The Waste Land* (1922) by T. S. Eliot (1888–1965) utilises the myths of the Holy Grail and the Fisher King, while *The Lord of the Rings* (1955) by J. R. R. Tolkien (1892–1973) uses a personal mythology that borrows heavily from a wide range of other traditional mythologies.

objectivity: an impersonal style of writing in which the author seems to be detached from his subject, presenting a balanced judgement rather than imposing his own personal views and preferences. Objectivity was highly fashionable in British poetry between about 1920 and 1950, largely as a reaction against what was seen as the excessive SUBJECTIVITY of late Romantic poetry (see p. 80). It is doubtful if any book or work is genuinely objective; some appear to be more so than others.

paradox: an apparently self-contradictory statement that on closer examination is shown to have a basis of truth. As well as illustrating a truth, a paradox concentrates the reader's attention on what is being said, through the initial shock of an apparently nonsensical statement, as in these last two lines of a poem from the *Holy Sonnets* by John Donne:

One short sleepe past, wee wake eternally,
And death shall be no more, Death thou shalt die.

parody: a work written in imitation of another work, usually with the object of ridiculing or making fun of the original.

pastoral: in general, literature that concerns country life. There are a number of pastoral conventions in literature. *As You Like It* (?1599) by William Shakespeare and *Lycidas* (1637) by John Milton (1608–74) are the two works with elements of pastoral in them that are most commonly set for 'O' and 'A' level examinations. For a more detailed discussion of the topic, read William Empson, *Some Versions of Pastoral* (1935) (see Part 7: Select Reading List).

personification: giving inanimate objects or abstract ideas human qualities or actions; making non-human things appear as human. The technique is seen most clearly in plays or poems where abstract qualities such as Lust, Lechery, or Greed are given human form and speech. The Pathetic Fallacy is a phrase which the student might come across which has links with personification. It refers to the tendency to describe Nature in human terms – something seen as pathetic, because it illustrates man's inability to face up to the fact that he is alone in the world, and a fallacy, because nature is not human in any respect.

realism: realism in literature is a source of debate and argument, at the heart of a number of schools and movements, and one of the most misused words in criticism. As a general guide, realism is the attempt to show life as it is, whereas idealism represents life as it should be. Because of the difficulties over this term, however, when a student writes that a book is 'realistic' – in the sense of giving an appearance of being close to life – he might be better advised to write 'naturalistic'. However, to add to the difficulties, the term 'Naturalism' refers to a specific nineteenth-century movement in literature.

satire: directing laughter at human vice, folly, and frailty. Satire can be light and amusing, or savage in the bitterness with which it exposes human wrongdoing; examples of both types of satire can be found in *Gulliver's Travels* (1726) by Jonathan Swift (1667–1745). One idea behind satire is that by exposing vice and folly to ridicule it renders it ineffective and harmless; a criticism of it is that it often destroys without suggesting positive alternatives to what is being criticised.

school: critics often refer to 'schools' of poets, or other authors, such as the Metaphysical poets (see p. 79) or the War Poets (see p. 81). These schools are a critical convenience, but should not be taken too seriously as strict definitions of what is in an author's work. A school of poets (or other writers) will have a number of features – stylistic, subject matter, or other features – shared between them; any single author is likely to have a certain number of these features, but rarely all of them at one time.

sentimentality: writing which calls forth an over-simplified, too easy volume of emotion from the reader. Sentimentality sees human nature as virtuous and without complexity. It has been described as 'emotion without intelligence' – an 'outpouring of emotion unimpeded by thought'. One of the best (or worst) examples of sentimentality is the death of Little Nell in *The Old Curiosity Shop* (1841) by Charles Dickens.

simile: see METAPHOR.

style: of the thousand and one meanings that this word can have, the simplest one is that it refers to the collective impression left by the way that an author writes; in other words, an author's manner of writing. An author's style is individual, a form of literary finger print.

subjectivity: subjectivity is a manner of writing which emphasises the author's personal response. Subjective works are often written in the first person, the 'I' mode, and appear as one individual's outlook or view. See also OBJECTIVITY.

symbol: a symbol is, like an image, something that stands for something else, but it is not merely descriptive. Literary symbols – the great white whale in *Moby Dick* (1851) by Herman Melville (1819–91), the lighthouse in *To the Lighthouse* (1927) by Virginia Woolf (1881–1941) – are multi-layered in their meanings. They convey a number of different messages, meaning different things to different characters in the books concerned, and different things to the reader. Very often a symbol has no specific meaning, just this collection of different meanings for different people.

theme: the central idea or ideas examined by a writer in the course of a book. Sometimes this idea is simply explored, its important details laid bare to the reader, but more often the writer presents certain conclusions on his theme or themes. A book's subject and its theme need to be distinguished; the subject is what the book is written about, its theme the author's ideas about that subject. As examples, the theme of *Our Mutual Friend* (1865) by Charles Dickens is money and its effect on society; its subject is the society of Dickens's day. The theme of Shakespeare's *Henry IV Part 1* (1598) is kingship, politics, and rebellion, whilst its subject is events in the reign of King Henry IV.

wit: a term which has gone through several meanings. It can mean intelligence or wisdom, or the application of these features to experience. It can be used in the sense of 'quick-witted', implying high imaginative powers on the part of an author, originality, and the ability to think quickly. It can mean excellence of judgement, a reasoned and balanced outlook. Its most modern meaning is of something intellectually amusing, often with a mildly shocking or surprising element in it.

Part 3

Drama

Talking points

Just as with prose and poetry, the writing of plays, or drama, has its own rules, conventions, and disciplines. The difference is that drama is always intended for performance in front of an audience. It is true that certain poetry, such as *The Canterbury Tales* (*c*.1387) by Geoffrey Chaucer, and even extracts from novels, as with Charles Dickens and his works, have been performed or at least read out in front of an audience; it seems likely that Chaucer's *Canterbury Tales* were written in the full knowledge that this is how they would be circulated. However, even though drama cannot claim to be unique in its 'live performance' aspect, it is certainly very different in this respect from most poems and novels.

Poetry and novels can be 'hard' for the student to master; drama is difficult in another sense altogether. The student studies a play from a written text; if he is lucky he may well see a performance of the play in question, but even if this does happen most of his knowledge will be acquired from a reading of the printed word on the page, rather than from actual performances. Right from the start this gives an air of unreality to the criticism of drama, because the student is reading something that was never designed to be experienced in this manner, but was meant instead to be experienced as a visual and oral exercise, something to be seen and heard rather than read. In some respects reading a play is similar to being an archaeologist who tries to decide what a dinosaur looked like with only the evidence of its bones in front of him. The words of a play are its bare bones, and the crucial thing about it, but they sorely need to be brought to life by actors, scenery, and music if the full experience is to be realised.

The artificial situation the student finds himself in can cause a number of problems. A minor one is where music plays a large part in the play, and the impact of this music has somehow to be allowed for or imagined by the student. There are a number of more serious problems. In a Shakespeare play, for example, the student can often fail to appreciate the significance of pomp, ceremony, and display in the play. A simple stage direction such as 'Flourish. Enter Claudius, King of Denmark, Gertrude the Queen, Councillors, Polonius and his son Laertes, Hamlet, cum aliis' is a bare statement of fact when written. On the stage, it translates into a blare of ceremonial music that can make the audience jump in their seats, followed by a glorious pageant of extravagantly dressed people streaming onto the stage in a blaze of colour and noise. The entry of the full court of Denmark is visually immensely exciting, but it is an effect that a mere reading of the play does not bring out. Nor does a bare reading bring out the vast contrast that exists between this scene and the one which immediately precedes it, with a few scared soldiers lost in the cold and fog of the castle's highest towers.

Another problem is that of identifying the characters. The reader of a play is told the names of whoever is speaking, but in the theatre he can see them and hear them, and so has much more than mere words on which to base his judgement and impression of their personality.

The major problem, however, is the so-called 'human element' in plays. A director and actors can take the bare text of a play and impose wildly differing interpretations on it. The text is not so much a strait-jacket as a loose and flexible mould (at least with some authors) which can be pushed and pulled by the director and actors into several different shapes. There are extremes, of course: Shakespeare is famous (or notorious) for the freedom which his plays allow directors and actors, while a play by George Bernard Shaw (1856–1950) tries to dictate every detail down to almost every last inflexion in the words.

As a general rule, the more modern the author, the more he will try to dictate in the text how his play is acted and performed. But even when an author gives clear instructions these are not always carried out. Unlike a poem or a novel, a play is not a finished article when its words have been printed on a page. It needs actors, directors, and a host of others to bring it to its peak, and the text is merely the starting point. Human beings are rarely perfect, and even the author sitting in at rehearsals and talking to the actors from the floor of the theatre does not ensure a perfect performance. As with music, where many famous works were met with little or no enthusiasm on their first performance, so with drama. Essentially mediocre plays have been turned into smash hits because, for reasons no-one can discover, a particular combination of director and actors created something special and unique. Similarly, plays destined to become classics have sunk almost without trace when first performed because the human element, vital to any play, failed to recognise or bring out the merits of the text. A play is not just words on a page; it depends for its success not merely on the author, but on an appallingly complex combination of people and talents, from the actors themselves down to the costume and set designer – and even the audience. There is a vital and live link between the actors and the audience in front of which they perform; no-one who has been to both a matinee and an evening performance of the same play by the same company, and seen the sometimes huge differences between the two performances, will deny this strange and insubstantial link.

Equally, the variable nature of plays should not be overestimated. The text is the base from which the play must proceed, and the crucial element in the success or otherwise of a play; but unlike the other two literary modes a play does not depend *only* on its words. This can create problems for authors, actors, and audiences; it can be a nightmare for the poor student. Examining boards do not allow for the human element that is present in drama. It is easy to sympathise with the student whose answer to the question 'Is Hamlet mad?' is that it all depends on how it is acted; the business of criticism does not allow for consideration of such subjective issues as this. When writing about a play, the student has to decide how it should be performed, and look at the play's *potential*. In a literary essay, every performance is perfect, the set never collapses, every actor comes in on cue. The student is writing about how the play should be performed in an ideal world, and giving the reader his vision of that perfection.

The main thing is that the student should have this vision of the play, and that he knows how it should be performed. There are certain general principles which help to achieve this aim.

The plays of Shakespeare are probably most open of any to differing interpretations. On a relatively minor level, someone studying *Hamlet* might have to write an essay on Gertrude, Queen of Denmark and Hamlet's mother, as a fairly crucial character in the play. Hamlet's father has been murdered by his brother, Claudius, who has taken over the crown, and married the ex-king's wife, Gertrude. The problem with Gertrude is to decide if she knows that her new husband is a murderer, which makes her a callous and immoral personality, or if she is unaware of what has happened, in which case she is merely a pliant and rather slow-witted woman. Any good actress can decide the issue very quickly on stage by the way she speaks and looks – by the exchange of knowing looks with Claudius or by showing a blank-faced smile in his presence. The text itself leaves it open. The student, however, has to reach his decision on the basis of the words alone, and also on the basis of the general development of Gertrude's character throughout the play, and the general scheme of ideas in the play. It has to be realised that a decision on one character affects other characters as well. It is no use having a view of Gertrude that sees her as a willing accomplice to murder, and a view of Hamlet that sees him as an immensely shrewd judge of character: Hamlet clearly does not think his mother knew of the murder, and so the views contradict each other. Almost the most common mistake made in writing about plays is this failure to see that characters in a play do not exist in isolation, and that a view of any of them must fit in with the view of all the characters in the play as a whole.

Characterisation

With the exception of a very few modern, experimental works, all plays have characters. Just as in a novel, a major task facing the author is to decide how his characters should be presented to the audience. Unlike a novelist, the author of a play cannot take the reader aside and tell him what to think about a character, or appear on stage and give a description of a character.

The simplest method of characterisation is by means of a character's actions and words – what he does and what he says. One way of giving an insight into a character's private thoughts is through a soliloquy, or monologue, where a character is alone on stage, speaking out loud to the audience. The problem facing the author here is one of realism; we tend to think our thoughts, not speak them out loud when alone, and a way round this problem is to provoke a character into saying what he or she thinks by putting them in a tense situation where we could believe that they lose their normal inhibitions. Exciting or tense situations do not occur in plays simply because they provide characters with an excuse to speak their thoughts.

As in a novel, we learn about a character from what he or she says, and also from the impact he or she has on other characters. Whereas it is sometimes a strain on realism to have a character talk out loud about himself, it is quite acceptable to show someone else talking about him, as anyone who has been the victim of gossip will realise. Look for points of characterisation not only in what the characters in question say, but also in what other characters say about them. It is here that a dramatist can bring into play one of his most subtle techniques: our image of a character is formed not only by what someone else says about them, but also by the character and personality of the person who is speaking. A big boost can be given to a character if the audience hear someone who has no reason to love the character speaking in his praise. When in *Hamlet* Claudius states that the people of Denmark love Hamlet, we know this to be an undeniable fact, that Hamlet can inspire love and respect from ordinary people; Claudius hates Hamlet, and so would never flatter him. An author can also create the opposite effect, by giving a speech in praise of a certain character to another character whom we dislike or find ludicrous. It is an extension of the traditional idea that a person should be judged by his friends, and those with whom he chooses to associate.

Imagery can play a vital part in forming our attitude towards a character. If a person's speech is laced with continual references to illness, disease, and decay, as Hamlet's is, then it does not take long for the audience to associate that character with these same features, either as a cause of them or a recipient. Macbeth's continual references to beasts of prey, blackness, and blood help the audience to see him as a dangerous and evil man.

Look out also for mannerisms of speech; an accent, as suggested by the spelling or stage directions, or a particular way of speaking, or continual use of certain words and phrases. Look out also for appearance. In an older play the only references to a character's looks may be in the text itself, with casual descriptions of a character's size, shape, or the clothes he wears.

In a novel character is often stated; in a play, it has to be deduced, largely from the words given to the character by the dramatist. In some cases, the process of deduction is not difficult, particularly when an author is creating so-called 'flat' characters; but for more complex characters only a thorough examination of their speeches, their reactions to the events of the play, the reaction of other characters to them, and their impact on the play as a whole, can result in a proper analysis of their nature and bearing.

Plot

A play's plot is its story, and as such it is the most menial and basic of the elements of a play. It is usually the lure by which the dramatist attracts his audience into the theatre and keeps them in their seats, whilst it is usually his themes or his characterisation (or in some cases, his language) that will win acclaim for the play as a work of art. The plot is therefore often no more than a means to an end, but it should not be underestimated. However grand an author's themes may be, if his plot is wrong and does not allow sufficient attention to be devoted to that theme, then the play will fail. There is considerable skill in linking up the various incidents in a plot, and maintaining suspense and tension right to the end. There are, therefore, as many areas of interest for the student in a play's plot as there are in other, perhaps outwardly more exciting areas, such as themes or characterisation.

One thing to look for is the existence of a sub-plot. A sub-plot is a secondary plot in a play, designed to provide variety and a change of scene from the main plot while at the same time keeping the audience in touch with the themes and concerns of the main plot. An excellent illustration of what a sub-plot should be can be found in Shakespeare's play *King Lear* (1606). Here the sub-plot and the main plot are carefully interleaved, in roughly alternating sequence, with the sub-plot examining the themes found in the main plot, but from a different viewpoint. So that the play is not split into two entirely separate works, certain characters and scenes combine both plots. At the climax of the play sub-plot and main plot join up, with the sub-plot brought to a conclusion just before the main plot, to allow the latter the whole stage.

A play which illustrates how gloriously a sub-plot can go wrong is Sir John Vanbrugh's *The Relapse*. The supposed main plot here concerns Loveless, a young man who has reformed and changed his sinful ways after marrying the pure and virtuous Amanda. Quite clearly the play starts off with the central idea of showing Loveless's 'relapse' from virtue by the contamination of his old ways. As a means of introducing breadth and variety there is a sub-plot, featuring Lord Foppington and his younger, penniless brother Young Fashion. The main plot proceeds to show Loveless's relapse, but the supposed sub-plot starts to occupy more and more scenes and take more and more of the play's interest from the main plot, as Young Fashion decides to marry the lecherous Hoyden, the rich daughter of Sir Tunbelly Clumsy, and the girl Lord Foppington intends to marry. This sub-plot is highly inventive, and has by far the most effective and comic character of the play in Lord Foppington. The result is that the play changes direction completely, concentrating on the sub-plot, and leaving the audience in considerable doubt as to what will happen eventually to the Loveless–Amanda relationship; indeed, Vanbrugh makes no attempt to answer this at the end of the play, which finishes firmly with the sub-plot. In a play that was never intended to be tightly constructed this mistake can be excused; in other plays a similar error or lack of control would split a play down the middle.

Some plays have parallel plots, rather than a main plot and a sub-plot. One example is Shakespeare's *Much Ado About Nothing*, in which the plot, which centres on the characters Hero and Claudio, provides the narrative interest and a comment on romantic love, while the plot which centres on Beatrice and Benedick provides the play's comedy, and its comment on real love.

Characters in a play are usually thought of as having lives which started before the action of the play; the events in a play are often influenced or dictated by things which happened before the action of the play starts. It is worth looking out for lines, or even whole scenes, designed to fill in background information that the audience needs before it can begin to understand what it sees. The opening scene of *Hamlet* is designed partly with this in mind, as is the opening exchange in *King Lear*.

Literary terms

Terms of general literary significance are dealt with in Part 2. As in the other sections on literary terms, the words in small capital letters in the definitions below are also to be found as headwords, with their separate definitions, in their appropriate alphabetical positions elsewhere in the list.

Absurd: Drama or Theatre of the Absurd was a term applied to a number
of dramatists in the 1950s. Though never a school in the accepted
sense of the word (see p. 30), these dramatists shared a belief that
human life was essentially irrational, purposeless, and out of
harmony with its surroundings, the result of this being a chronic state
of uncertainty, anguish, and depression. Other authors had reached
this conclusion before; none had allowed it to dictate the *form* of their
plays as well as its *content*. Absurd plays drop all logic and rationality,
allowing absurd, irrational, and illogical things to happen on stage in
order to illustrate their central thesis that this is the nature of life.
Though mild by comparison with many later plays, Samuel Beckett's
(*b.*1906) *Waiting for Godot* (1953) shocked theatre audiences at first
by its absence of plot or structure, its bare set, and its central concept
that 'nothing happens'. Some writers in the Theatre of the Absurd are
Edward Albee (*b.*1928), Samuel Beckett, Eugene Ionesco (*b.*1912),
Arthur Adamov (1908–70), Jean Genet (*b.*1910), Harold Pinter
(*b.*1930), and N. F. Simpson (*b.*1919).

Angry Young Man: a phrase that derives from the character Jimmy
Porter in the play *Look Back in Anger* (1956) by John Osborne
(*b.*1929); it applies to the generation of young people brought up in
the 1950s in Great Britain who were in revolt against the social system
as it then was, but had no real alternative to replace it. See also
KITCHEN SINK DRAMA.

apron stage: a stage or acting area that juts out into the auditorium,
leaving the actors surrounded by audience on three sides; sometimes
called a *thrust stage.*

blank verse: poetry based on a metrical structure (a repeating pattern of
stressed and unstressed syllables) which does not rhyme. Shakespeare
is perhaps the most famous user of blank verse, although Christopher
Marlowe (1564–93) was the first major dramatist to pioneer its use.
Shakespearian blank verse usually has five stressed syllables per line,
though the structure is mostly very loose.

catharsis: the Greek scientist and philosopher Aristotle (384–322BC)
defined catharsis in his *Poetics* as the proper effect of TRAGEDY: a
purging of the emotions of pity and fear from the audience by their
presentation on stage. By removing these emotions, at least tem-
porarily, tragedy performed a useful social function, inasmuch as
the emotions might be harmful if left in place. The term now is used of
the 'draining' of emotion that the audience feel at the end of a tragedy.

Chorus: in the classical theatre the Chorus was a group of actors on stage
throughout the performance who provided a running commentary on
it. Shakespeare introduces a Chorus into *Henry V*, but by this time it
has become a single figure whose sole job is to fill out details in the
audience's mind, and who is only on stage at irregular intervals.

comedy: in its original sense, a play with a happy ending. Nowadays it means a play that makes the audience laugh, but in the Elizabethan period it was customary to classify plays as comedies by their endings, rather than their humorous content.

director/producer: often confused, but technically speaking the director of a play is responsible for its artistic content, for rehearsals, and for guiding the actors, while the producer is responsible for raising finance and generally seeing to the administrative, business side of the production.

farce: a type of comedy, made popular in France in the nineteenth century, and usually containing the following elements: a series of complex and intricate plot situations which appear irreconcilable until cleared up as if by magic by the author; flat or stock characters, the comedy coming from the situations the characters are placed in rather than from the complexity or interest of the characters themselves; a sexual or amatory content; an element of slapstick, knockabout, or physical humour. There are strong elements of farce in plays written before the nineteenth century, but these plays would normally be referred to as comedies.

Globe Theatre: an Elizabethan theatre made famous by being the place of the first performance for many of Shakespeare's plays. A reconstruction of the theatre, showing the recognised features of the Elizabethan Theatre, is given on p. 40.

'kitchen sink drama': a type of play associated with John Osborne's play *Look Back in Anger* (see ANGRY YOUNG MAN). 'Kitchen sink drama' usually refers to plays with a true-to-life, rather seedy setting and action.

masque: a lavish form of dramatic entertainment relying heavily on song, dance, and costumes, with extravagant spectacle and special effects. The genre flourished in the first half of the seventeenth century in England, having been imported earlier from Italy. Ben Jonson probably ranks as the greatest of masque writers. The masque most familiar to examination candidates is *Comus* (1634) by John Milton.

melodrama: now a derogatory term, melodrama is sensational, highly emotional, full of excitement but with little depth of characterisation, and usually has a happy ending. Very popular in the late nineteenth century in England, there are still many plays which use elements of melodrama. One of the most famous of all melodramas was *Sweeney Todd, the Demon Barber of Fleet Street*, which exists in three versions; modern texts usually combine elements of all three texts.

Miracle Plays/Mystery Plays: these plays marked the high point of medieval drama, reaching a peak in the fourteenth and fifteenth centuries. The plays were essentially dramatisations of episodes and scenes from the Old and New Testaments of the Christian Bible. They

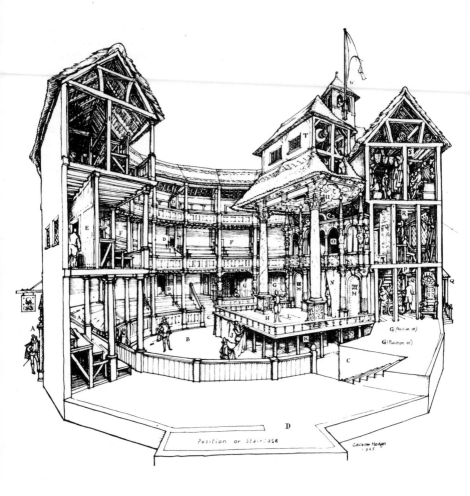

A CONJECTURAL RECONSTRUCTION OF THE INTERIOR OF THE GLOBE PLAYHOUSE

AA Main entrance
 B The Yard
CC Entrances to lowest gallery
 D Entrance to staircase and upper galleries
 E Corridor serving the different sections of the middle gallery
 F Middle gallery ('Twopenny Rooms')
 G 'Gentlemen's Rooms' or 'Lords' Rooms'
 H The stage
 J The hanging being put up round the stage
 K The 'Hell' under the stage
 L The stage trap, leading down to the Hell
MM Stage doors

N Curtained 'place behind the stage'
O Gallery above the stage, used as required sometimes by musicians, sometimes by spectators, and often as part of the play
P Back-stage area (the tiring-house)
Q Tiring-house door
R Dressing-rooms
S Wardrobe and storage
T The hut housing the machine for lowering enthroned gods, etc., to the stage
U The 'Heavens'
W Hoisting the playhouse flag

were presented from a wagon, complete with complex stage effects and the actors; a whole 'cycle' of plays would be performed in one location before the company moved on to the next. The most famous cycles were York (forty-eight episodes), Coventry (forty-two), Wakefield (thirty-two), and Chester (twenty-five). The cycles tended to become the property of the town which held them. They were so demanding, in terms of both resources and time, that the trade guilds of the time (a cross between a modern trade union and a professional association) took over responsibility for the plays, each guild mounting a particular episode. Thus the ship-builders' guild might mount the episode of Noah and the Flood, the nail-makers the Crucifixion, and so on. The term 'Mystery Play' comes from the tendency of these guilds to refer to their crafts as mysteries, perhaps to enhance the respect with which they were viewed by the populace.

Morality Plays: the successor to Miracle and Mystery Plays, Morality Plays were simpler, and mounted on primitive stages, rather than on wagons. For a description of *Everyman*, a morality play, see p. 23, under 'allegory'.

prompt copy: the prompter is the person paid to remind actors of their lines when they forget them on stage. A prompt copy is the copy of the play used by the prompter, and because of its special use it will have certain notations in it that will differ from the normal acting copy, such as details of when actors pause naturally in their speech, or when special effects are mounted, so that the prompter does not give an unnecessary prompt. Some of Shakespeare's plays are thought to have been printed from a prompt copy.

proscenium arch: the standard 'picture frame' stage, or a stage where the action takes place largely behind a square arch over the stage area. Compare APRON STAGE.

Restoration Comedy: the Restoration period, from 1660 to the early eighteenth century, produced both comedies and tragedies; with a few notable exceptions, only the comedies have been remembered. With only a small number of theatres in London at the restoration of Charles II, and with the audience for drama much more restricted to upper social classes than it had been in Shakespeare's time, the nature of the plays being written and performed changed. Restoration Comedy deals almost exclusively with the affairs of the upper classes; it is graceful, heavily concerned with sexual behaviour, and places a huge premium on wit as the most acceptable social virtue. Best-known authors are William Congreve (1670–1729), William Wycherley (1640–1716), Sir George Etherege (1634–91), George Farquhar (1678–1707), and Sir John Vanbrugh.

Revenge Tragedy: the name given to a whole style of writing associated with the Elizabethan period. The first great revenge tragedy was *The*

Spanish Tragedy (1592) by Thomas Kyd (?1558–?94), and large numbers of others were to follow, the most famous of all being Shakespeare's *Hamlet*. Revenge tragedy had, obviously, revenge at the heart of its plot. Revenge was popular because it allowed for a dramatically stimulating contradiction between an individual's strong and understandable desire for revenge, and the fact that Christianity condemned personal revenge as a grave sin. As well as this moral dilemma, revenge as a plot also gave an excuse for murder, adultery, rape, incest, suicide, and general bloodbaths, all of which the average audience found highly entertaining. By having evil purged at the end of the play (usually the revenger dies along with those he is revenging himself against) the dramatist could also claim to be writing something morally worthy, while at the same time having given his audience the thrill of seeing a great deal of evil on stage. Well-known examples of revenge drama are *The Revenger's Tragedy* (?1606) by Cyril Tourneur (?1575–1626), *The Jew of Malta* (?1590) by Christopher Marlowe, and *The Duchess of Malfi* (?1614) by John Webster (?1580–?1634).

set: the scenery or background against which a play is acted.

soliloquy: a long speech in which a character, usually alone on the stage, expresses his thoughts out loud.

tragedy: Greek tragedy developed from ancient rituals; Elizabethan and Jacobean tragedy developed from Greek tragedy and a host of other influences; modern tragedy – if such a genre exists – has developed in turn from these and many other influences. No single definition of tragedy is possible, except perhaps to say that a tragedy is a play with an unhappy ending – but even this simplest of definitions hardly comes near to defining the complex emotional and intellectual pattern that marks out a play as being tragic.

The Greek scientist and philosopher Aristotle (see CATHARSIS) said that tragedy had to be serious, wide in its scope, and complete in itself. For him the tragic hero was high-born, and neither particularly evil nor particularly good, but merely normal in his balance of the two. Due to some tragic flaw – a weakness or mistake on his part – the tragic hero goes from happiness to misery and death. Later authors defied these rules and yet produced something very recognisable as tragedy. Shakespeare's Macbeth is evil, and there is a small element of comedy in the play (as there is in all Shakespeare's tragedies); this renders the play not a tragedy according to Aristotle's rules, but the play is clearly a tragedy, whatever he may have said. It has been a matter of much debate whether or not tragedy is possible in the modern theatre. Modern attempts at tragedy have tended to make the tragic hero low-born rather than an aristocrat. Examples include *Death of a Salesman* (1949) and *The Crucible* (1953) by Arthur Miller (*b*.1915), and *Juno and the Paycock* (1924) by Sean O'Casey (1880–1964). One area where Aristotle probably was right was in saying that tragedy aroused the twin emotions of pity and terror or fear in the audience, and then purged them; pity and fear seem to be an element in all plays with tragic overtones.

tragi-comedy: a play that is a mixture of tragedy and comedy; a play where the characters do not die, but are brought sufficiently near to it to stop the play being classified as a comedy.

History and reading list

The basic aims behind this combined reading list and literary history are explained in the introduction to this handbook.

Group 1: Greek drama; Miracle, Mystery, and Morality Plays

This is an unlikely combination of plays, combining as it does classical times and medieval times. Both sets of plays exerted significant influence on later drama, of the type that is set on modern examination syllabuses; both sets of plays appear on conventional reading lists, and occupy prime positions in histories of literature. However, neither set of plays is necessary for an 'O' level student or equivalent, and is necessary only to the most committed of 'A' level students. The reason for this is simply that these plays, of either group, never themselves appear on examination syllabuses, and so their interest to the examination candidate consists primarily in the influence they have exerted on later drama, most notably Shakespearian and Elizabethan drama.

For further background to this group, see entries under CATHARSIS, TRAGEDY, MIRACLE PLAYS/MYSTERY PLAYS, and MORALITY PLAYS in the 'Literary Terms' section above.

Reading list
TEXTS:
Sophocles, *Oedipus Rex.*
Everyman.

Group 2: Shakespeare

Remarkably little is known about William Shakespeare, certainly England's most famous dramatist, and perhaps the most famous dramatist ever to have lived. He was born the son of middle-class parents in Stratford-upon-Avon in 1564, and moved to London where he became involved as a writer and actor in the theatre, notably with the company of actors known as the Lord Chamberlain's Men. He seems to have retired to Stratford in 1610, having written or part-written thirty-six plays and a number of poems. He married a girl called Anne Hathaway in his youth, possibly after having made her pregnant, and scholars have debated at length the fact that at his death in 1616 he left to his wife his 'second best' bed.

No-one can be absolutely certain that the plays attributed to Shakespeare were actually written by him, although attempts to prove other authorship have by and large failed. Two other complicating factors have to be added. Firstly, authors frequently collaborated in order to write plays in Shakespeare's time, or had what they wrote altered either by actors or other writers. Secondly, the absence of any copyright laws meant that authors in Shakespeare's time were reluctant to publish their plays, as this made the performance of them by rival companies very easy; the result was 'pirated' or unreliable issues of the text of plays, or, in the case of Shakespeare, publication some time after his death, with no evidence that the author had the opportunity to prepare his texts for the printers. Most of the plays attributed to Shakespeare (and all the great ones) were almost certainly written by him; the texts as we have them are, it would seem, largely accurate, with a few notable exceptions; that is about the limit of what can be said.

For the examination candidate Shakespeare's work falls into a number of recognisable categories, roughly as follows:

(a) *Early plays (1585–1590)*
Richard III is occasionally set for examinations. It is somewhat clumsy, rather long-winded, but nevertheless an attractive mixture of part black comedy, part history, and part tragedy.

(b) *History plays (1590–1600)*
Shakespeare wrote a number of history plays, but the most popular ones are those referred to as the 'second tetralogy' – *Richard II, Henry IV Part I, Henry IV Part II, Henry V*. These plays examine the state of England, and in particular its political structure with regard to the all-important issue of kingship. Roughly speaking, *Richard II* examines a king who has the right to rule, in terms of his being the lawful king, but not the skill or character. The Elizabethans, and people of later ages, believed that kingship came from God by means of the hereditary principle, and that it was one of the greatest crimes that a man could commit to murder a king or remove him from his throne. Thus a bad king presents a basic moral dilemma if he holds his throne legally with God's apparent consent. The next play, *Henry IV Part I*, shows the noble Bolingbroke who usurps the throne from Richard, and eventually has him killed. Henry IV, as he is now known, is a good military leader and a religious, fair man. In a practical sense he has many of the skills and features of a good king, but he is the direct opposite of Richard: while Richard II had

the right but not the skill or ability, Henry IV has the skill and the ability but not the right. In *Henry IV Part I*, and in *Henry IV Part II*, Henry IV faces continual rebellion and trouble from within his state, troubles which eventually lead to his death. However, his son, Henry V, has succeeded to the throne by process of inheritance from his father, and is therefore a legal king, not a usurper. He has the right to be king, and he has the skill. The result is shown in the play *Henry V*, in which Henry triumphs over his enemies, both internal and external, and leads England into a golden age. The four plays thus show a progress towards the concept of the ideal king, typified by Henry V.

Henry IV Part I and *Henry IV Part II* also contain Falstaff, one of the greatest comic creations of all time. Falstaff represents the malaise that consumes England under the reign of a usurper, Henry IV, and which threatens the next king, Henry V. A huge barrel of a man, he has every disease under the sun; he is a thief, a lecher, selfish, a boasting braggard, a parasite. But Falstaff is also extremely amusing, possessed of a huge energy or life force, and, in his way, completely honest; he makes little or no secret of what he is, and indeed seems to delight in it. He represents Misrule, or anarchy, in the society which Henry V has to govern, and Henry V, as Prince Hal, has to learn to reject Falstaff, however attractive his carefree way of life might seem.

Henry V is usually presented as a straightforward celebration of England and its hero-king. Some recent productions have emphasised the element of sacrifice there is in Henry V, the sacrifice of his own personality and wishes to the all-embracing demands of kingship.

(c) Comedies (1590–1600)
Shakespeare wrote a number of comedies, although some of them are quite serious in tone and mood. The four best-known comedies are probably *Twelfth Night, As You Like It, Much Ado About Nothing*, and *A Midsummer Night's Dream*. Both comedies and tragedies have at their heart the 'appearance and reality' theme, a concern firstly with self-knowledge, and secondly with how one distinguishes between what a person or situation seems to be, and what it actually is. The difference between comedy and tragedy in Shakespearian terms is as follows: in both comedy and tragedy a character can have inadequate self-knowledge and inadequate knowledge of the real nature of other people, but in tragedy the character is likely to be destroyed by this lack of knowledge and awareness, while in comedy he is allowed to learn from his mistakes and survive. Orsino in *Twelfth Night* thinks he is in love when he is not (it is simply the idea of being in love that he likes), and fails to recognise the real thoughts of the characters who surround him. Lear in *King Lear* similarly thinks people love him when they do not, and does not know enough about his own personality and responses. Orsino gets happily married; Lear dies in horrific circumstances. It can be seen

from this that though comedies tend to end happily, they do have a serious element in them, and are not merely vehicles for frothy laughter. There are intensely moving moments in all the comedies, as well as hilarious ones, and in most comedies one character is left out of the charmed circle of happiness at the end (Malvolio in *Twelfth Night*, Jaques in *As You Like It*, Don John in *Much Ado About Nothing*) to remind the audience that happiness is not always the result of human endeavours, and that things do not always work out to everyone's convenience.

(d) Tragedies (1600–1608)
Probably Shakespeare's most famous plays, the four 'great' tragedies, and the most significant, are *Macbeth, Hamlet, King Lear,* and *Othello.* Other famous tragedies frequently set in examinations are *Julius Caesar, Romeo and Juliet,* and *Antony and Cleopatra.* Shakespeare's tragedies are based in part on classical, Greek models, part on his own invention, and part on the fashions and influence of his own time. They usually feature someone of high or noble birth, or at least someone who is eminent in his own society, such as Othello. That person is usually an attractive personality with many virtues, and a fairly normal balance of good and evil within them. They have, however, a tragic flaw or weakness which allows the powers of evil to lure them into trouble and eventually destroy them. Macbeth's tragic flaw is that he is ambitious, Hamlet's that he thinks too much, Lear's that he is proud and does not know himself, and Othello's that he is jealous. All these features are ones which we ourselves might think we have; part of the tragedy is that these 'normal' faults are so acted on by events in the play that they bring the hero down.

Evil is let loose in the society of the tragedy, and destroys both good and evil characters. Often it pollutes or infects the tragic hero himself. There is usually at least one recognisable source of evil in the play; Claudius in *Hamlet*, the Witches in *Macbeth*, Edmund, Goneril, and Regan in *King Lear*, and Iago in *Othello*. Tragedies are thus partly a demonstration of the age-old battle between good and evil in society. The lesson we learn is that evil will eventually burn itself out, destroy itself, but not before great damage has been done. At the end of the tragedy evil has been purged, society cleansed, and things can go back to normal under a regenerative figure such as Fortinbras (*Hamlet*) or Malcolm (*Macbeth*), the tragic hero having died in the purging process. Shakespeare's tragedies mix tragedy and comedy, and in the case of Macbeth have an evil man as tragic hero. They owe their success partly to the power with which they are written, but also to the feeling they give of being representative, making a statement about human nature and the nature of existence which applies to all humanity. In particular the tragedies look at the forces controlling man – gods, Destiny, Fate,

Providence, or any one of a number of other names – and their relationship with him. These forces, and negative powers within the hero himself, usually destroy the tragic hero, after he has been put to an immense amount of anguish, suffering, and stress. Rather than depressing the audience this can hearten and encourage them; the battle against Fate is one that mankind is bound to lose, but the mere fact that man can carry on the fight, hopeless as it might be, and that he can simply endure what he has to undergo, is almost comforting, arousing our feeling of pride in man, and enhancing our respect for his courage and bravery.

(e) Problem comedies (1600–1608)

A cynical critic may say that the problem with the so-called problem comedies is that they are not very good. Be that as it may, the problem comedies do exist – *Troilus and Cressida*, *Measure for Measure*, and *All's Well That Ends Well* – and of the three *Measure for Measure* is the one most often set in examinations. The problem with these plays is that there is a great deal of bitterness, upset, and turmoil in them, so that the happy endings are unconvincing, or do not seem to fit in with the atmosphere of the play as a whole. *Measure for Measure* starts off as a tragedy, and then changes tack completely; at the climax of the play Angelo, the villain who has attempted firstly to seduce Isabella, and then to pervert the course of justice in order to murder her brother, is suddenly forgiven and marries Mariana. The problems of these plays go deeper than can be suggested in a short note such as this, but they are also plays that have a considerable power and attraction of their own. It is possible to view them as experiments on the road to the next group, the dramatic romances.

(f) Romance plays (1608–1611)

This group is usually considered to consist of *Pericles*, *Cymbeline*, *The Winter's Tale*, and *The Tempest*. Apart from some plays doubtfully attributed to Shakespeare and some collaborations, *The Tempest* was the last play written by him. Of these plays *The Winter's Tale* and *The Tempest* are the most frequently set for examinations. They are comedies in the sense that they have partially happy endings, but they also partake heavily of elements found in both the histories and tragedies. In one sense they are the triumph of Shakespeare's art, plays which blend the comic, historic, and tragic visions of life by means of a vast human sympathy and a belief in the healing powers of time.

Reading list

TEXTS:

If you are studying a single play, you should try to read as many as possible of the plays that are in the same group, as detailed above. If you want a good general knowledge of Shakespeare, or wish to compare a comedy with a tragedy, then the plays which are most representative, most interesting, or easiest to read (and sometimes all three at the same time) are probably *Henry IV Part I, Twelfth Night, Hamlet, Measure for Measure*, and *The Tempest*.

CRITICISM:

More books have been written on Shakespeare than on any other single author. The list which follows is the briefest of possible lists, containing only the most basic reading. Details of the publisher and date and place of publication for these books are given in Part 7: Select Reading List.

Always remember that reading the texts is much more useful than reading criticism.

A. C. Bradley, *Shakespearian Tragedy*. Old-fashioned, narrative, far too willing to see the characters as real people instead of fictional creations, Bradley's book is still the critical classic, with a huge range of insights into the four great tragedies. Bradley helped to found modern literary criticism, and this book is still one of the most helpful and informative ever written on Shakespeare.

H. B. Charlton, *Shakespearian Comedy*. A rather unexciting but basically helpful commentary on Shakespearian comedy.

J. Dover Wilson, *The Fortunes of Falstaff*. The basic critical work on the second tetralogy of history plays.

H. Granville-Barker, *Prefaces to Shakespeare*. Another early, pioneering book, and an excellent introduction to Shakespeare's work particularly as it is now widely available in relatively cheap paperback editions.

E. M. W. Tillyard, *Shakespeare's Problem Plays*. Somewhat hostile to the problem plays, but useful and effective criticism nevertheless.

E. M. W. Tillyard, *The Elizabethan World Picture*. A short but highly effective and informative introduction to Elizabethan thought patterns, with particular reference to the way in which the Elizabethan era differed from the modern day in the way people thought.

Group 3: Elizabethan and Jacobean drama

No-one has ever really explained why the thirty years from 1580 to 1610 saw one of the greatest flowerings of drama that have ever taken place in English literary history, and probably in the history of world literature. Shakespeare was only one part of this boom in drama, and perhaps not even the author most highly thought of by the age in which he lived. The reasons for the development of the Elizabethan and Jacobean theatre are complex, part social, part political, part economic, and with a host of other influencing factors. It is not the suddenness of this growth, nor the quality of its authors, that is perhaps the most significant feature, but rather the fact that the Elizabethan and Jacobean theatre was the first *professional* theatre in England, in the modern sense, performing in purpose-built theatres to a paying audience, and with actors who made their living from their trade. That same thirty years was to see vast changes in the theatres themselves, and in the type of plays they presented. Early theatres were partly open-air and therefore lit by natural light; but indoor theatres with a wider range of technical effects were becoming common by the end of the period (Shakespeare's play *Cymbeline* (1611) is one of the first to include demands for special effects that seem designed with an indoor theatre in mind).

Certain things, however, did not change throughout the period. Sets or background were largely static, and the audience's impression of place conveyed not by painted flats or backdrops, or complex structures on stage, but by words and by costume (look at the way that an actor will often tell or describe where he is to someone else on stage at the start of a scene, so the audience do not feel lost). Furthermore, women were still not permitted to act, and female parts were taken by boys specially trained for this task. It is generally assumed that these boy actors were able to master very complex portrayals of female parts.

The theatres were closed in 1642 as part of the English Civil War, and remained closed until 1660 and the restoration of the monarchy, but signs of decadence had been visible much earlier, possibly even as early as 1615; from the mid 1620s to 1642, drama seemed to have little new to offer. Again, no-one has ever really explained why this flowering of drama should wither and die as suddenly as it had blossomed.

Thomas Kyd (?1558–?94) has already been mentioned as the author of *The Spanish Tragedy* (1592), a play which seems to have exerted a significant influence on the development of REVENGE TRAGEDY (see the 'Literary Terms' section above). More famous, and more interesting, is Christopher Marlowe (1564–93). It seems almost certain that he was a spy for the British government while studying at Cambridge in his youth. He came to London and had a runaway success with his *Tamburlaine the Great* (?1587), written in two parts. Marlowe's magnificent use of blank verse in this play exerted a vast influence on other authors and plays, and together with *The Spanish Tragedy* it can probably claim to be the most influential of all Elizabethan/Jacobean plays. He then went on to write *The Jew of Malta* (?1590), *Doctor Faustus* (?1591), and *Edward II* (1592), all of which are still performed with some frequency nowadays. Marlowe died when he was stabbed to death in a brawl over who should pay a bill for a meal, but this apparently simple incident covers a wealth of suspicion and mystery. Throughout his life

Marlowe seems to have been involved with almost every vice conceivable, from homosexuality to devil worship (though nothing was ever proved), and a number of theories have been raised about his death. One theory has it that he was killed on the orders of the government, afraid that he might reveal state secrets; another claims that he did not die at all, but fled under cover of his false death to France where he proceeded to write the plays attributed to Shakespeare.

Another author as famous in his day as Shakespeare was Ben Jonson (1572–1637), a bricklayer, soldier, and actor who wrote several excellent plays, and who became perhaps the most skilful writer of the MASQUE (see 'Literary Terms' above) in English literary history. His comedies, notably *Every Man In His Humour* (1598), *Volpone* (1606), and *The Alchemist* (1610) are better known than his tragedies. Though not as mysterious as Marlowe, his life was certainly not dull, including spells in prison and a walk from London to Edinburgh, in Scotland. At his best Jonson's ability to write sharply satirical comedy and well-constructed plots puts him on a level with the best English dramatists.

The fame of John Webster (?1580–?1634) rests on two plays, both in the revenge vein: *The White Devil* (?1608) and *The Duchess of Malfi* (?1614). He wrote a number of other plays which have since been lost. His plays are full of violent action, and are obsessed with evil. While individual scenes and the poetry of certain lines are very strong, his plays hold together less well than Shakespeare's, and sometimes can appear as individual scenes with little to connect them. He wrote a large number of other plays in collaboration with other authors.

Cyril Tourneur (?1575–1626) probably wrote *The Atheist's Tragedy* (1611) and *The Revenger's Tragedy* (?1606), and it is the latter play on which his reputation rests. There is a quite strong body of opinion which attributes *The Revenger's Tragedy* to the author Thomas Middleton (1580–1627). Either way, the play itself is a horrific yet partly comic vision of evil and wholesale corruption, with its central revenger, Vindice, typical of a whole class of character.

Other well-known authors include Francis Beaumont (?1584–1616), John Fletcher (1579–1625), George Chapman (1560–1634), Thomas Dekker (?1572–?1632), John Marston (?1575–1634), and John Ford (1586–?1639).

Reading list

TEXTS:
Marlowe, *Doctor Faustus*.
Jonson, *The Alchemist*.
Kyd, *The Spanish Tragedy* or Tourneur, *The Revenger's Tragedy*.

CRITICISM:
Una Ellis Fermor, *The Jacobean Drama*.

Group 4: Restoration Comedy

The English monarchy was restored to its throne in 1660, after several years of rule by Oliver Cromwell and the Commonwealth. The new king, Charles II, had spent most of his period of exile in France, and had developed a taste for drama while there. When he returned a change in style of drama was inevitable. Fourteen years of neglect had made the old theatres (some ten or fourteen of them in London) of the Jacobean period unusable; the old acting companies had dispersed; developments on the continent, imitated by what little drama had been possible under Puritan, Commonwealth rule in England, had given rise to a taste for more elegance, richness, and show in drama, to the extent that even Shakespeare was considered barbarous, and had to be re-written in order to suit the taste of the day.

The theatres therefore changed. There were only two theatres for the early part of Charles's reign, and both – Covent Garden and Drury Lane – survive today on almost the same sites as they had all those years ago. They cost a great deal more to build than the Jacobean theatres, and were much richer and more ornate, with PROSCENIUM ARCHES (see 'Literary Terms' above) and sliding flats to enable scene changes to take place against a backdrop of exciting painted flats. The actors changed, with young women acting the female parts for the first time, there being no young boys with the necessary training. The plays and the audience changed. The audience was now rich, upper-class, young, cynical, and fashionable, at least until the end of the century, and the plays were written to match this audience. Sexual intrigue and the antics of high-born London society featured largely in the plots of the new plays. There was tragedy in the dramatic repertoire as well as comedy, but the tragedies of the period have not survived the test of time as well as the comedies. Indeed, there are only two tragedies from the Restoration period that are likely to be staged by a modern theatrical company, *All For Love* (1678) by John Dryden (1631–1700) and *Venice Preserv'd* (1692) by Thomas Otway (1652–85).

The comedies valued WIT (see Part 2: Literary Terms in General Use) above all other features, perhaps as a result of a society with wealth and time on its hands: with no radio or television, the ability to be entertaining counted very high amongst social virtues, and witty people were entertaining, if nothing else. Certain stock characters and certain stock themes became common in the comedies. There was the fop or dandy (the man obsessed by his appearance and social status, and a fool as well), the young rake (a young, fashionable man with plenty of charm and little money, usually morally unscrupulous but destined to marry the heroine), the country bumpkin (an uneducated countryman made a fool of by the town people, or sometimes the other way round), the immoral young woman, the sexually frustrated, licentious middle-aged or old woman, and the pure young woman of unblemished reputation. A common theme was the position of the younger son or sons of a well-to-do family. The law dictated that all the estate and inheritance of a man of wealth went to the eldest son, and the younger sons (necessary to continue the line in case the eldest son died) were given a small annuity or pension, and left to fend for themselves, often by entering into the church, or joining the army. These younger sons, with the breeding of a rich person and his tastes, but none of his money, are at the heart of many restoration comedies. Women also come in for serious consideration, and in particular the system of arranged marriages. In those times a girl married for economic and political reasons, and was quite lucky if these coincided with love. Married for money, both husband and wife could still be left with an unfulfilled need for love, both physical and mental, and this could be supplied by a lover or a mistress. It was one reason why many European societies of the time allowed the King's mistress a semi-official position; he of all people had little freedom in whom he married, and needed the solace of a mistress.

The comedies, therefore, tended to develop a morality of their own, one in which good looks, wit, and the ability to adapt with ease and skill to the highly sophisticated demands of top society counted for more than the older virtues of sobriety and morality. This trend continued unchecked until the replacement of the morally lax Stuart monarchy by that of the much more puritanical, sober, and cautious William III in 1688. The year 1688 marked a turning point, although it was several decades before this became apparent. In Charles's time the theatre had been for the rich upper classes; in William's time, it became much more open to invasion by middle-class audiences, and these audiences were not prepared to accept the same degree of immorality as were the older clientele. Under the twin pressure of monarchy and audience, drama did what it has always done, and produced what the audience wanted, which turned out to be an altogether quieter and less daring type of play. The symbol for this change in taste was a pamphlet produced by the Reverend Jeremy Collier (1650–1726), called *A Short View of the Immorality and Profaneness of the English Stage* (1698). The pamphlet roundly condemned the theatre of the day for its immorality.

Nowhere can the change in taste be better seen than in a comparison between the two plays, *The Relapse* (1696) by Sir John Vanbrugh (1664–1726) and *The Beaux' Stratagem* (1707) by George Farquhar (1678–1707). *The Relapse* has two plots; in one a faithless husband escapes without any obvious punishment, in the other a young rake is allowed to marry the rich woman his brother intends to marry, and live happily ever after. Thus in both plots what by conventional standards is immorality is rewarded, and the audience's sympathy lies, if anything, with the characters who are most sinful in conventional terms. Farquhar's play seems set on the same trail. Two young men from London with excellent manners and no money go to a provincial town in order that one of them should attract and marry a rich young woman. The woman, of course, will have to be deceived into thinking that the young man is rich (they plan to do this by one of the men pretending to be his own brother, who is a noble lord); when they are married by law the woman's wealth will become the property of the man. Almost at the very last minute the young man confesses his trick, finds he is actually the noble lord he has been impersonating (his brother has suddenly died), and so marries the young woman with a clear heart and spotless morality. His friend is also allowed to marry a woman he was on the verge of seducing. The content of the two plays is much the same – money, seduction, high life – but the endings are different: *The Beaux' Stratagem* can offend no-one – unless, of course, they look at what *almost* happened, and what is only averted by a series of huge coincidences that lack genuine credibility.

Other authors of the period who have achieved fame are William Wycherley (1640–1716), Sir George Etherege (1634–91), and William Congreve (1670–1729). Wycherley was a master of satire, sometimes savage, and there is a dark edge to the humour in his plays, the best-known of which are *The Country Wife* (1675) and *The Plain Dealer* (?1674). Etherege is more robust, though still with a strong satirical edge; his best-known play is *The Man of Mode* (1676). The title of greatest Restoration dramatist must go to William Congreve. He wrote a number of plays including *The Double Dealer* (1694) and *Love for Love* (1695), but his greatest triumph, and arguably that of the whole Restoration period, was *The Way of the World* (1700). It was badly received when first performed, and has a plot which is so complex and intricate that it is almost incomprehensible (so much so that the actors in rehearsal for the first performance are reputed to have gone to Congreve to ask him to explain what was happening); nevertheless in its wit, style, and elegance it is a major achievement. Its character insight, particularly into the female psychology, is deeper than in any contemporary play, and in the characters of Lady Wishfort and Millamant it contains respectively one of the funniest and one of the most compelling characters of all time. There is a feeling of rush and hurry to much Restoration comedy, hardly surprising in the case of a play such as *The Relapse* which was written in six weeks in order to get a friend out of debt. There is none of this in *The Way of the World*, as elegant (and funny) a comedy as has ever been written.

After the first few years of the eighteenth century, drama as a whole loses the excitement, invention, and gaiety of the Restoration period, and enters into a long period of depression.

Reading list
TEXTS:
Congreve, *The Way of the World.*
Farquhar, *The Beaux' Stratagem.*
Vanbrugh, *The Relapse.*

Group 5: Goldsmith and Sheridan

At the risk of making an over-sweeping generalisation, the eighteenth century contained little of significance in the way of drama. There were numerous reasons for this. After a hundred years as the leading literary genre (with only a brief respite in the middle of the century) it was perhaps time for a change. Increasingly restrictive censorship of the stage pushed promising writers into novel writing or poetry where perhaps before they might have made a career as dramatists. Irrespective of censorship, the novel and poetry were in a process of expansion, as more and more people became able to read and so provide a market for published poetry and prose.

Two authors emerge from this rather blank period to feature still on examination syllabuses. Oliver Goldsmith (1730–74) is probably better known as a novelist or poet than as a dramatist, but he did write *She Stoops to Conquer* (1773), a play which has remained a firm favourite with amateur companies in particular. The play is a comedy, owing perhaps more to Farquhar than any other dramatist. The plot is highly improbable, the play highly amusing: Restoration comedy without the coarseness, and with some exceedingly accurate observation of human nature in its comic mode. The role of Tony Lumpkin has been a favourite one for comic actors virtually since the play was written.

A rather more telling dramatic talent was Richard Brinsley Sheridan (1751–1816), who spent relatively little time as a writer, being drawn away from this to the richer pastures of theatrical management and politics, in both of which spheres he enjoyed a successful career. His three best-known plays are *The Rivals* (1775), *The School for Scandal* (1777), and *The Critic* (1779). His plays are witty, well constructed, and often satirical in their humour. He is a master of theatrical effects, using the physical resources of staging and set to create comedy. Perhaps he is most remarkable for his ability to be wholly honest about the people he portrays, yet to provide at the same time an atmosphere of gaiety and bubbling wit which robs his plays of any malice. The works of both Goldsmith and Sheridan are sometimes referred to as simply weaker versions of Restoration comedy, an allegation that is perhaps more true of Goldsmith than it is of Sheridan. Sheridan does have a talent and style that is all his own, though it has obvious links with the earlier style of drama.

Reading list
TEXTS:
Goldsmith, *She Stoops to Conquer.*
Sheridan, *The School for Scandal.*

Group 6: Shaw and Wilde

If the eighteenth century was a slack period for drama, then the nineteenth century was even worse. Until mid-way through the century the two original theatres of the Restoration period, Covent Garden and Drury Lane, had a monopoly of the theatre which proved to be extremely unhealthy. Audiences and the government lacked imagination and a taste for inventiveness, and there were a host of other reasons for this relative decline, most of which are beyond the scope of this handbook. The dramatist who did set the pace was not British, but the Norwegian Henrik Ibsen (1828–1906), often regarded as the father of modern theatre. Ibsen is naturalistic and realist in his early plays, and symbolic in his later plays; it is the symbolic richness of his plays that has made the greatest impact on modern audiences and critics. His major works are *Brand* (1865), *Peer Gynt* (1867), *A Doll's House* (1879), *An Enemy of the People* (1882), *Ghosts* (1881), and *The Wild Duck* (1884). This last play marks the start of Ibsen's symbolic phase, which culminated in *John Gabriel Borkman* (1896) and *When We Dead Awaken* (1899). His impact on realism in the theatre can be gauged by the subject matter of his plays, which included municipal corruption, venereal disease, and truth and falsehood in marriage.

The first major talent to make itself heard for many a year in the British theatre was Oscar Wilde (1856–1900). Wilde's career was cut short by his arrest, conviction, and imprisonment for homosexual activity, but before this he had written, among other works, the two plays on which his fame as a dramatist rests: *Lady Windermere's Fan* (1892), and *The Importance of Being Earnest* (1895). The plays have a subject matter and theme which is verging on the commonplace, but their overriding and dominant feature is their verbal dexterity and wit, an unequalled ability to turn words into comedy and satire. Wilde's word-play is both amusing and sharp, attuned to comedy and characterisation as well as to comic effect. In addition to his verbal dexterity and ability to coin memorable phrases, Wilde had a passion that verged on self-destruction, and the wildness, wit, and individuality of his life has brought him at times to the status of a cult figure. However, the revival of British drama owes more to George Bernard Shaw (1856–1950) than to any other dramatist. As a drama critic Shaw formed strong ideas on the nature of drama, and was heavily influenced by Ibsen's work. Shaw followed Ibsen's lead in cultivating greater realism and naturalism in his work, with results that sometimes caused his plays to be banned; this was the fate of *Mrs Warren's Profession* (written in 1893 but not staged until 1902) which dealt with prostitution. Shaw's best-known plays are *Arms and the Man* (1894), *The Devil's Disciple* (1897), *Major Barbara* (1905), *Man and Superman* (1901–3), *Pygmalion* (1913), *Heartbreak House* (1920), *Back to Methuselah* (1918–20), and *Saint Joan* (1923). Shaw was a left-wing theorist, a man of ideas, and a vastly stimulating personality and author. The prefaces to his plays are almost as long as the plays themselves, and Shaw is sometimes accused of using his characters merely as a vehicle for his ideas, losing reality of characterisation in the process. Although Shaw's plays can be overladen with his ideas, this is usually more than compensated for by his wit, his comic invention, and his ability to shock an audience with his reasoned unconventionality. A number of features have guaranteed Shaw's survival as a dramatist, both in critical terms and on the stage. Shaw was an excellent technician, with both a great respect and a great knowledge of theatrical form and play construction. He is highly original, delighting in particular in taking a conventional type of character and turning it inside out, and revealing the new version as the truth. Thus the armaments manufacturer in *Major Barbara* is shown to be the saviour of society, whilst the supposedly good characters are shown as canting and ineffectual hypocrites. Shaw looks at the basic issues of human existence in their most serious aspects, but he also has a wit and infectious gaiety that invite comparison with Congreve, or Wilde. This combination of serious intent with comedy is not unique (good comedy has always had a serious side to it), but the particular blend as used by Shaw is entirely his own. By bringing Ibsen's blend of controversial realism and symbolism into drama in England Shaw did British drama a great service. If Shaw and Wilde were the brightest stars on the authorial stage other developments should not be overlooked, notably those in staging. Victorian drama, particularly in the last third of the nineteenth century, had tended towards spectacle and vast effects requiring considerable expense. Increasingly towards the end of the old century and the start of the new one the author's wishes began to be taken seriously, and the staging of classics, such as plays by Shakespeare, began to be marked by closer attention to historical detail. The process was a lengthy one, but the pruning of the excesses of the theatre can be said to have started at the turn of the century.

Reading list
TEXTS:
Wilde, *The Importance of Being Earnest.*
Shaw, *Heartbreak House.*

Group 7: T. S. Eliot and verse drama

T. S. Eliot (1888–1965) is better known as a poet than as a dramatist. Nevertheless his plays, notably *The Cocktail Party* (1949) and *The Family Reunion* (1939) are still set by major examination boards occasionally. On one level they reflect a resurgence in the art of verse or poetic drama that reached its high point with *The Family Reunion*. The attraction of verse drama was partly its use in the Elizabethan period by such authors as Shakespeare. It was thought that this period represented the last age in which high intellectual ideals had been combined with popularity in literature, with its appeal to a wide audience. However, Eliot added to this noble ideal two further ideas of his own – a strong religious faith, coupled with the desire to convert his audiences to Christianity, and a willingness to base his plays closely on classical predecessors. As verse plays, religious plays, and plays based on classical examples, Eliot's work has considerable interest. As drama, probably only *Murder in the Cathedral* can stand in its own right, and even then it performs much better in the church than in the theatre.

Reading list
TEXT:
Eliot, *Murder in the Cathedral.*

Group 8: Modern British drama

Although there were extremely competent playwrights working in the 1930s and 1940s, very few, apart from T. S. Eliot, ever make their way on to the examination syllabuses. It was in the mid-1950s that the next great flowering of British drama took place, a flowering which made drama the dominant literary genre for at least twenty years. It is worth asking why there was such a long blank period for drama from the end of the Restoration period to the time of George Bernard Shaw, almost two hundred years. One answer is that drama is much more at the mercy and control of its audience than either the novel or poetry is at the control of readers. A novel or book of poems can be published, sell a few copies, and then lie dormant, even for years, until fashions change and the author in question is seen as thoroughly acceptable. If a play is a failure on its first night, more often than not it is doomed with almost immediate effect. Theatre is often a middle- or upper middle-class activity, and for years the inherent conservatism of audiences acted like a dead weight on drama, pulling it down to a level of repetitive unoriginality. In the mid-1950s authors found the courage to shock their conventional audiences, and to write what they, the authors, wanted to write, rather than what the audiences wanted to hear. This new, dramatic writing sprang, however, from a society where theatre was becoming more widely available, and where education was helping to produce vocal and literate young writers from all classes. As always in these movements and fashions a complex process of economic, social, political, and moral patterns combined to produce a given effect – in this instance a flood of daring young dramatists with a great deal to say (not that all of it was worth saying), and the theatres which allowed them to say it.

It is possible to discern two separate strands in the dramatic revival that took place in the mid-1950s, although certain authors tend to appear in both camps. Possibly the most influential play written in the twentieth century is Samuel Beckett's (*b.*1906) *Waiting for Godot* (1953); as with most of Beckett's work this was written first in French. Beckett is an Irishman who eventually settled in Paris, France. *Waiting for Godot* was a vast shock to the theatre audiences who saw it in the mid-1950s. Large numbers of people walked out of the theatre in disgust, Beckett was accused of being a theatrical fraud, and only one major critic in England – Harold Hobson, then writing for *The Sunday Times* – hailed the play as a masterpiece. The play has two tramps, Vladimir and Estragon, waiting – on a stage bare except for a leafless tree – for the arrival of a mysterious personage called Godot. In some unexplained way the arrival of Godot will make everything better. Godot never comes. Instead, a bullying tyrant of a man, Pozzo, appears, with his slave Lucky, and a young boy enters to say that Mr Godot will not come today, but will come tomorrow. The second act follows much the same pattern, with a few alterations. Vladimir and Estragon are still waiting, but the tree now has a few leaves on it. Pozzo and Lucky enter, but this time Pozzo has gone blind, and Lucky is leading him on a rope; a young boy comes on and gives the same message as in the first act. The play is a tragic farce. Perhaps its most surprising element is that it is very funny, and can arouse considerable sympathy for the two clown-like tramps. It is tempting to see the play as a satire on religion, but it goes deeper than that, and any interpretation of it as a straightforward ALLEGORY (see Part 2: Literary Terms in General Use) is wrong. The play became a cornerstone of the Drama of the ABSURD (see 'Literary Terms' above). Beckett's other plays become progressively more obscure and unactable, although *Endgame* (1957) can actually hold an audience and provide a worthwhile evening. As a symbol of much of Beckett's other work, *Come and Go* (1965) runs for only three minutes and contains only one hundred and twenty-one words of dialogue.

A writer manifestly influenced by Beckett, but with a voice very much his own, is Tom Stoppard (*b.*1932). He made his name with the play *Rosencrantz and Guildenstern Are Dead* (1967), which examines the lives of the two Shakespearian characters (Rosencrantz and Guildenstern both appear in Shakespeare's *Hamlet*) while the action of *Hamlet* is taking place around them. The links with *Waiting for Godot* are clear: both plays are tragi-comedies; both have two rather amiable central figures lost and wholly confused in the midst of a world which they do not understand, cannot influence, and which seems essentially hostile to them. In this sense Stoppard is writing very much in the vein of the Drama of the Absurd, presenting an essentially illogical vision of the universe, and pitying in comic manner the poor human beings caught up in it. Stoppard has written numerous other plays, a number of which reflect growing concern for political oppression and the victims of totalitarian societies, and a movement away from the Absurdist mode of writing. Firmly in this mode are *Jumpers* (1972), *The Real Inspector Hound* (1968), and *Travesties* (1974). Other plays include *Professional Foul* (1977) and *Every Good Boy Deserves Favour* (1977).

Harold Pinter (*b*.1930) is another author whose works are allied to the Theatre of the Absurd, and it is sometimes claimed that Pinter is the greatest living British dramatist. His three best-known plays are *The Birthday Party* (1958), *The Caretaker* (1960), and *The Homecoming* (1965). Early Pinter plays tend to show characters hiding or living within a small, well-defined area, which represents security and safety, with the feeling of a potentially hostile outside world waiting at the fringe, ready to burst in. This security and safety are always destroyed, and the phrase 'comedy of menace' has been coined to describe the atmosphere and style of plays such as *The Birthday Party* and *The Caretaker*. As with all plays that owe anything to the Absurd movement, the plays are funny, but the humour is tinged with menace, particularly since the characters usually end by being denied the security for which they crave.

The second wave of mid-1950s dramatists is best represented by John Osborne (*b*.1929). Osborne's *Look Back in Anger* (1956) added two phrases to the vocabulary of drama, the ANGRY YOUNG MAN and 'KITCHEN SINK DRAMA' (see 'Literary Terms' above). The hero of the play, the angry young Jimmy Porter, came to represent a whole generation of young people who felt that they had no say in the running of a society that was corrupt and rotten, and which was in effect run by those older than themselves entirely in their own interest. The language of the play is colloquial and rough, the setting is naturalistic, and the strident voice of protest is very audible. *Look Back in Anger* can be seen now as one of the first salvoes fired in the battle to gain young people a place and influence of their own in society, and which lead directly to the youth culture and rebellion of the 1960s. Osborne's career as a dramatist has been troubled, but *Luther* (1961) and the savagely satirical *Inadmissible Evidence* (1964) are generally held to be successful plays.

Arnold Wesker (*b*.1932) invites comparison with Osborne as a major dramatist, although here as well it is probably true to say that Wesker's later work has not tended to reach the same standard as his earlier plays. Wesker's best-known plays are *Chicken Soup with Barley* (1958), *Roots* (1959), *I'm Talking About Jerusalem* (1960), and *Chips With Everything* (1962). There is a strong social element in Wesker's work, as well as considerable comic ability and an eye for effective theatrical presentation.

Another leading figure in the 'new wave' of dramatists is John Arden (*b*.1930), whose reputation rests largely on one play, *Serjeant Musgrave's Dance* (1959). Arden is one of the relatively few British dramatists to be heavily influenced by Bertolt Brecht (1898–1956), the German poet and dramatist, and this influence can be seen to be working in *Serjeant Musgrave's Dance*. Arden's unwillingness to draw neat and tidy thematic conclusions from the experience he presents in his plays, and his tendency to mix verse and prose, has given rise to a mixed reception from critics and audiences. He is still a major talent, perhaps the most underestimated dramatist of his time.

Reading list
TEXTS:
Beckett, *Waiting for Godot.*
Stoppard, *Rosencrantz and Guildenstern Are Dead.*
Pinter, *The Birthday Party.*
Osborne, *Look Back in Anger.*

CRITICISM:
Martin Esslin, *Drama of the Absurd.*

General critical reading on the theatre

Theatrical history is well documented. A very useful, well illustrated history of the theatre is Phyllis Hartnoll's *A Concise History of the Theatre*. Another useful reference work is John Russell Taylor's *A Dictionary of the Theatre*.

Practical criticism and appreciation

There are essentially two types of essay questions on drama texts: the one in which the student is asked to comment on a passage from a play he already knows and on which he has done some work, and the 'unseen' passage, where the student is presented with a passage he has never seen before, and asked to write intelligently on it. If anything, the first type of question is easier, partly because the student should already know something about the passage in question, and partly because a question on a text already studied frequently asks something specific, rather than giving a general directive to discuss the passage. The 'context question' usually asks the student to state where a passage comes in a play; to translate certain phrases or lines; and to answer questions on the passage – what the passage achieves, what it tells the reader about a certain character, and so on. The unseen 'comment and appreciation' or 'practical criticism' passage is usually more open-ended, simply asking the student to write an appreciation of the given passage, or requesting a discussion of its style and technique.

For convenience a specimen answer to both types of question is given below.

1. Context question

(a) Translate the following passage into clear modern English.
(b) What does this passage tell us about Hamlet's state of mind at this point in the play?

> HAMLET: To be, or not to be: that is the question.
> Whether 'tis nobler in the mind to suffer
> The slings and arrows of outrageous fortune
> Or to take arms against a sea of troubles,
> And by opposing end them. To die, to sleep—
> No more—and by a sleep to say we end
> The heartache, and the thousand natural shocks
> That flesh is heir to! 'Tis a consummation
> Devoutly to be wished. To die, to sleep—
> To sleep—perchance to dream: ay, there's the rub,
> For in that sleep of death what dreams may come
> When we have shuffled off this mortal coil,
> Must give us pause. There's the respect
> That makes calamity of so long life:
> For who would bear the whips and scorns of time,
> Th' oppressor's wrong, the proud man's contumely,
> The pangs of despised love, the law's delay,
> The insolence of office, and the spurns
> That patient merit of th' unworthy takes,
> When he himself might his quietus make
> With a bare bodkin? Who would fardels bear,
> To grunt and sweat under a weary life,
> But that the dread of something after death,
> The undiscovered country, from whose bourn
> No traveler returns, puzzles the will,
> And makes us rather bear those ills we have,
> Than fly to others that we know not of?
> Thus conscience does make cowards of us all,
> And thus the native hue of resolution

Is sicklied o'er with the pale cast of thought,
And enterprises of great pitch and moment,
With this regard their currents turn awry,
And lose the name of action.—Soft you now,
The fair Ophelia!—Nymph, in thy orisons
Be all my sins remembered.

(a) *Advice*: Translating into clear, modern English is known as *paraphrasing*. It can sometimes be surprisingly difficult. The student has to bring out fully the meaning of the passage set, but at the same time make the passage sound completely modern in its style and phrasing. Normally a question on a passage such as this would ask only for selected lines and phrases to be translated, but to give a fuller example of paraphrase, the whole passage is translated here.

Answer:

To be, or not to be: that is the question.
Whether 'tis nobler in the mind to suffer
The slings and arrows of outrageous fortune
Or to take arms against a sea of troubles,
And by opposing end them.

PARAPHRASE: Should I do what I need to do, or should I not? That is the issue that has to be decided. Is it better to submit to the blows and agony that life inflicts without logic or reason, or to make a stand against a mass of troubles, and by fighting back end them? (This is a very difficult passage, because Hamlet believes that if he does take action it will result in his own death. Does the student translate the surface meaning, or what Hamlet is implying? The safest answer is to do both: write out the translation as given, but add as well something like 'Alternative: Is it better to submit and live, or fight and die?').

To die, to sleep—
No more—and by a sleep to say we end
The heartache, and the thousand natural shocks
That flesh is heir to!

PARAPHRASE: To die, like a long sleep, to be no more – and by this sleep to imagine that we bring to an end the anguish and the pain that are inseparable from being alive, and which humans are born to suffer.

'Tis a consummation
Devoutly to be wished. To die, to sleep—
To sleep—perchance to dream: ay, there's the rub,
For in that sleep of death what dreams may come
When we have shuffled off this mortal coil,
Must give us pause.

PARAPHRASE: It is a conclusion or outcome to be fervently prayed for. (The passage has 'devoutly', and the idea of religious devotion has to be expressed in the translation.) To die, to sleep, and then perhaps to dream: now there's a difficulty or obstacle. The dreams or nightmares that might come to us when we are in the sleep of death, and have shaken off the turmoil of this present life, must make us hesitate.

> There's the respect
> That makes calamity of so long life:
> For who would bear the whips and scorns of time,
> Th' oppressor's wrong, the proud man's contumely,
> The pangs of despised love, the law's delay,
> The insolence of office, and the spurns
> That patient merit of th' unworthy takes,
> When he himself might his quietus make
> With a bare bodkin?

PARAPHRASE: That is the consideration that makes the calamity of our lives last so long (*Alternative*: makes us reluctant to end our lives by suicide). Otherwise, who would suffer the insults of this world, the tyrant's cruelties, the proud man's attempts to humiliate those beneath him, the heartbreak of being in love with someone who does not return the emotion, the inevitable slowness of the law's working, the arrogance and rudeness of those who hold official positions, and the insults which good, patient people take from those who are less worthy, when a simple dagger could release him from life?

> Who would fardels bear,
> To grunt and sweat under a weary life,
> But that the dread of something after death,
> The undiscovered country, from whose bourn
> No traveler returns, puzzles the will,
> And makes us rather bear those ills we have,
> Than fly to others that we know not of?

PARAPHRASE: Who would bear burdens, complaining and sweating under the weight of life's cares, if it were not for the fact that fear of something coming after death, the unknown territory from where no traveller returns, confuses the intellect, and makes us prefer the troubles that we know about, rather than hurry towards ones that we do not know.

> Thus conscience does make cowards of us all,
> And thus the native hue of resolution
> Is sicklied o'er with the pale cast of thought,
> And enterprises of great pitch and moment,
> With this regard their currents turn awry,
> And lose the name of action.

PARAPHRASE: Thus conscious thought and reflection make cowards out of all of us, and so the natural colour of resolution is made to look pale and ineffectual by reflection and thought, and business of great height and importance when considered in this way goes off course and loses its sense of direction, becoming inactive.

—Soft you now,
The fair Ophelia!—Nymph, in thy orisons
Be all my sins remembered.

PARAPHRASE: Gently now, the beautiful Ophelia! Young woman, remember my sins when you say your prayers.

Conclusion: Basic principles of the paraphrase can be seen from the above. It is essential that the student keeps as close to the original syntax (sentence structure) as is possible, given that the paraphrase must be fluent and make sense. The examiner needs to be able to check the translation of individual words; the student has to convey the sense of a passage – its wider implications, as well as its exact meaning.

(*b*) *Advice*: The second part of the question asks specifically about what is learnt of Hamlet's state of mind from this soliloquy. The student who has studied *Hamlet* has to be careful not to bring in irrelevant information when answering a question of this nature, and stick to what is asked. An answer might read as follows:

Answer: The speech opens with a question, and there are two other extended questions in the passage, all of which suggests that Hamlet is undecided, and either unable or unwilling to make up his mind. Hamlet appears to be contemplating suicide. His comments on human life suggest that his vision of it is one of suffering, anguish, and pain. Hamlet's reason for people's failure to commit suicide is a cynical one, being simply that people are frightened that worse things await them after death.

When the speech opens its metre is broken and jagged, again suggesting uncertainty and confusion, but it becomes more ordered as the speech proceeds. Hamlet appears to take solace and comfort in explaining away the situation he finds himself in, perhaps suggesting that he calms his fears by apparently rational thought. In some respects Hamlet is describing himself when he states that 'conscience does make cowards of us all'.

Hamlet's imagery centres on pain and suffering, suggesting man in continual pain. His final reference to Ophelia might also suggest a man tortured by a sense of guilt, an awareness of his own sins. Therefore this soliloquy suggests that Hamlet is unable to make up his mind, contemplating suicide, and disenchanted with the suffering of human life. He is cynical, but comforts himself with reflection, even though he is clearly suffering greatly and aware of his own sins and weakness.

Conclusion: The answer given is brief and strictly relevant, working through the passage line by line, and tying it all up at the end with a brief conclusion. Questions of this nature rarely require a lengthy answer; the one that is short and to the point usually scores the highest marks.

2. Comment and appreciation question

Comment in any way that seems suitable on the passage given below.

> *The light suddenly fails. In a moment it is night. The moon rises at back, mounts in the sky, stands still, shedding a pale light on the scene.*
> VLADIMIR: At last! (*Estragon gets up and goes towards Vladimir, a boot in each hand. He puts them down at the edge of stage, straightens and contemplates the moon.*) What are you doing?
> ESTRAGON: Pale for weariness.
> VLADIMIR: Eh?
> ESTRAGON: Of climbing heaven and gazing on the likes of us.
> VLADIMIR: Your boots. What are you doing with your boots?
> ESTRAGON: (*turning to look at the boots*). I'm leaving them there. (*Pause.*) Another will come, just as ... as ... as me, but with smaller feet, and they'll make him happy.
> VLADIMIR: But you can't go barefoot!
> ESTRAGON: Christ did.
> VLADIMIR: Christ! What's Christ got to do with it? You're not going to compare yourself to Christ!
> ESTRAGON: All my life I've compared myself to him.
> VLADIMIR: But where he lived it was warm, it was dry!
> ESTRAGON: Yes. And they crucified quick.
> *Silence.*
> VLADIMIR: We've nothing more to do here.
> ESTRAGON: Nor anywhere else.
> VLADIMIR: Ah Gogo, don't go on like that. Tomorrow everything will be better.
> ESTRAGON: How do you make that out?
> VLADIMIR: Did you not hear what the child said?
> ESTRAGON: No.
> VLADIMIR: He said that Godot was sure to come tomorrow. (*Pause.*) What do you say to that?
> ESTRAGON: Then all we have to do is to wait on here.
> VLADIMIR: Are you mad? We must take cover. (*He takes Estragon by the arm.*) Come on.
> *He draws Estragon after him. Estragon yields, then resists. They halt.*

ESTRAGON: (*looking at the tree*). Pity we haven't got a bit of rope.

VLADIMIR: Come on. It's cold.

He draws Estragon after him. As before.

ESTRAGON: Remind me to bring a bit of rope tomorrow.

VLADIMIR: Yes. Come on.

He draws him after him. As before.

ESTRAGON: How long have we been together all the time now?

VLADIMIR: I don't know. Fifty years perhaps.

ESTRAGON: Do you remember the day I threw myself into the Rhône?

VLADIMIR: We were grape-harvesting.

ESTRAGON: You fished me out.

VLADIMIR: That's all dead and buried.

ESTRAGON: My clothes dried in the sun.

VLADIMIR: There's no good harking back on that. Come on.

He draws him after him. As before.

ESTRAGON: Wait.

VLADIMIR: I'm cold!

ESTRAGON: Wait! (*He moves away from Vladimir.*) I wonder if we wouldn't have been better off alone, each one for himself. (*He crosses the stage and sits down on the mound.*) We weren't made for the same road.

VLADIMIR: (*without anger*). It's not certain.

ESTRAGON: No, nothing is certain.

Vladimir slowly crosses the stage and sits down beside Estragon.

VLADIMIR: We can still part, if you think it would be better.

ESTRAGON: It's not worth while now.

Silence.

VLADIMIR: No, it's not worth while now.

Silence.

ESTRAGON: Well, shall we go?

VLADIMIR: Yes, let's go.

They do not move.

CURTAIN

Advice: This passage is from *Waiting for Godot* by Samuel Beckett, a play discussed earlier in this section. If the student knows the text from which an extract is taken then it is worth mentioning the fact in the opening lines of the answer. If not, try to place the passage at least roughly in terms of age and style, as below:

Answer: The passage appears to be taken from a modern play, possibly of the Drama of the Absurd school of writers.

This passage is a dialogue between two characters, Vladimir and Estragon. Stage effects are minimal, but the sudden failure of the light and equally sudden rising of the moon has a comic element to it which may have been intended by the author. The two characters speak to each other in a succession of brief, alternating lines: the longest speech is only five lines. The conversation itself is very varied. It can be commonplace ('What are you doing?'), poetic ('Pale for weariness'), religious ('Christ did'), philosophical ('We've nothing more to do here'), and personal ('Are you mad? We must take cover'). The language is simple and unadorned, for the most part.

The two characters seem to have known each other for a long time. Vladimir suggests they might have known each other for fifty years (although without a great deal of conviction or certainty), and the way they speak to each other is familiar (Vladimir uses a nickname, Gogo, to refer to Estragon). They reminisce about times past, and show concern for each other, but nothing they say appears to have very much effect, and they never remain on one topic for any length of time. It is almost as if their conversation had been used up many years ago, and they were just going through the motions of talking without really ever communicating. Both characters appear ineffectual, something emphasised by the last lines of the extract and the stage direction which follows ('Well, shall we go?/Yes, let's go. *They do not move*').

There appears to be a religious theme in the passage. Estragon compares himself to Christ who went barefoot, but the real significance of Christ for the two characters seems to be firstly that where he lived it was warm (the fact that Vladimir and Estragon are both cold is referred to several times in the passage); and secondly that in Christ's day 'they crucified quick', suggesting that Vladimir and Estragon are being slowly tortured to death, in a harder way than Christ's. A second reference that might be religious is to Godot, who is apparently coming tomorrow, and whose arrival will, according to Vladimir, make everything better. It is possible that the author is referring here to people's religious beliefs which allow them to suffer misery and misfortune in the hope that religion will produce something that will suddenly make things satisfactory, or better. If so the suggestion would appear to be that people are wrong to wait in this manner, but should, rather, act on the basis of what they know to be true. On the other hand the fact that someone has said Godot will come could be seen as a valid reason for awaiting his arrival.

An atmosphere of chronic indecision is created by the passage. Its theme might be stated as 'nothing is certain'; it seems that the two characters on stage are certain of nothing except their coldness, and the existence of each other. Anything else, from what they should do to whether or not they should remain friends, or were mistaken in becoming friends, is shrouded in uncertainty and indecision.

The passage seems to present a picture of two people alone against the world, uncertain about what they should do, and even about what they are. Their relationship is the only sure thing they have, yet even that seems to be automatic and unthinking, more a question of habit and apathy than a conscious choice on their part to be friends. Both characters are frozen by inertia, lack of motivation, and lack of confidence. Their relationship is partly comic and partly tragic. Religion appears to be a theme in the passage, although the exact nature of what is being stated about religion is unclear and ambiguous.

Conclusion: As with any essay of this type, the above answer is only one of many that might be written, all of which could have validity. The answer shows that the writer is prepared to make educated guesses about the 'meaning' of the passage, but is not afraid to admit to uncertainty; as much time is spent on style, technique and characterisation as on themes. The essay is based firmly on the set passage, not on a view of the play as a whole – an essential feature of all answers of this type.

Part 4

Poetry

Talking points

Poetry is often thought of as the most 'difficult' of the three literary modes or genres. Whilst this was true of a certain period of poetry in recent times, it is certainly not true of poetry in general. The early ballad form of poetry was mass entertainment for an unsophisticated audience; the poetry in Shakespeare's plays appealed to all sectors of society; numerous poets in the twentieth century have sold more copies of their poems than famous novelists have of their best-selling novels. Poetry can be obscure, and it can be hard to understand, but so can plays and novels; no one mode of literature has a monopoly of either complexity or obscurity.

If poetry is thought of as being complex, it is partly because of the writings of certain authors, partly because of its use of several specialised techniques, and partly because it tends to condense and compress experience and comment, making it perhaps the most concentrated form of literature. This tendency to concentrate, refine, and condense experience can make it tight-packed, and therefore harder to appreciate at first reading. We can watch a play while half-thinking about something else, and still grasp the basic concepts and plot sequences that the play is presenting. We can glance through a novel with half an eye on a television set, and still retain a vague idea as to what is taking place. When we read poetry, we can do nothing else. It is a full-time occupation, and of all the literary modes poetry demands the most concentration. Perhaps this is why it sometimes seems more difficult; it cannot be read lazily, and demands complete involvement. The other modes need this, but can still go some way with only partial involvement and concentration. This demand on concentration is one of the strengths of poetry: poetry can say and mean more, in a shorter space of time, than any other literary form, but it demands its price from the reader.

Poetry suffers from another drawback; the term 'poetic' can mean 'artificial', a suggestion that somehow experience is being twisted out of its true shape, and heightened or enlarged to an unreal extent. In some senses at least poetry is artificial. It uses the techniques of metre, rhyme, diction, imagery, and rhythm to enhance what it is attempting to say, and its language and style are often furthest removed from the language of everyday speech of all the literary modes. However, a great deal of poetry is also written in colloquial language, and an author such as Shakespeare can make blank verse (see p. 76) sound remarkably true-to-life and naturalistic. A student's initial reaction to poetry will often depend on the style and type of poetry with which he has been familiar up to that moment in his non-examination reading. Remember that poetry can take time to get used to, but the rewards of taking that time can be great.

Metrical structure/metre

All language has its own natural rhythm. Words are composed of syllables ('when' has one syllable, 'where/fore' has two, 'trag/e/dy' has three, 'mag/ni/fic/ent' has four) and in ordinary speech we stress one or more of these syllables. Try pronouncing 'tragedy' normally: you will place the stress on the first syllable, and say it TRAGedy. We learn these stresses instinctively when we are children, from our parents and those around us; if we are learning a foreign language, we learn them from books and from hearing people speak. Whichever way the knowledge is acquired, it is as basic a part of a language as the meaning of the words themselves, and cannot be ignored.

All language has a natural rhythm composed of stressed and unstressed syllables. To confirm this all that has to be done is to speak into a cassette recorder with the record function operating; the needle or light display which shows the sound input will peak or jump at certain moments when you are speaking; this is related as much to the stresses you are placing on a word as it is to the sound volume when you pronounce it.

Metre is a division of rhythm. A poet takes the natural rhythms that exist in language and disciplines, organises, and uses them in consistent, repetitive patterns to enhance what he is trying to say. The poet will select a certain type or kind of rhythm, depending on the atmosphere and tone of the poem he wishes to write; he will then fit his language round this rhythm and repeat it throughout the poem. When a rhythm is standardised and consistent or repetitive (that is, when the same pattern of rhythm is repeated throughout a poem) then it ceases to be mere rhythm and becomes metre.

Metre is classified according to its various types and categories. This classification is often a source of much confusion to students. The words used to classify metre are complex and unusual, and identifying the metrical structure of a poem can be difficult. But the actual principles on which metre is based are not difficult; if the student can persuade himself at least of that he will win through to an understanding of metre.

The first source of classification is the actual pattern of stressed and unstressed syllables that is being used in a poem. Each 'unit' of metre, each individual example of a particular pattern, is called a foot. When the student 'scans' a poem (reads through in order to ascertain its metre) he first has to decide which type of foot (individual pattern of stress) is being used. He is helped (in theory at least) by the fact that the most commonly used feet are quite few in number. A poem is usually composed of one of four feet; these can be marked by using two symbols, ˘ for an unstressed syllable, and — for a stressed syllable.

iambic: has a ˘ — pattern, as in **ŭnrēst, dĕfēat**

trochaic: has a — ˘ pattern, as in **wēlcŏme, ēmptў**

anapaestic: has a ˘ ˘ — pattern, as in **măsqŭerāde, sĕrĕnāde**

dactylic: has a — ˘ ˘ pattern, as in **wīllĭnglў, mērrĭlў**

It would be normal to find whole poems written in groups of one of the above feet. Sometimes, of course, an author cannot fit all he wants to say into the metre he is using; or perhaps he merely wishes to vary the metre. In either event he may use what are known as *occasional feet*; one of these might occur in a line of poetry, but a whole line or poem would not usually be based on them:

spondaic: has a — — pattern

pyrrhic: has a ˘ ˘ pattern

amphibrach: has a ˘ — ˘ pattern

Only assume that one of these feet is being used if all else fails.

Before the student can classify a poem's metre he has to complete one more task, that of deciding how many feet there are in a line of poetry. The classification of metre gives the type of foot first, and the word signifying the number of them in a line second. The terms are:

monometer:	one foot
dimeter:	two feet
trimeter:	three feet
tetrameter:	four feet
pentameter:	five feet
hexameter:	six feet
heptameter:	seven feet
octameter:	eight feet

Thus a poem might be said to have been written in iambic pentameters, a trochaic tetrameter, or a dactylic hexameter. Do not let the long words confuse you; they are describing something essentially quite simple.

There is only one way to scan a poem, or find out if it has a metrical structure, and if so, what it is. You have to read the poem, and as you do so listen to yourself and mark down the stressed syllables. When you start to do this you will find it difficult, in all probability, and put artificial stress on words where you would not dream of doing so under more normal and relaxed circumstances. The thing to do is to have your scansion checked by an expert, to see where you went wrong, and then keep on trying. Progress is usually very fast if the student is persistent. Here are some examples:

Ĭ grān̄d/ĭndēed/thăt fiēlds/ănd flōcks/hăve chārms

Fŏr hĭm/thăt grāz/ĕs ōr/fŏr hĭm/thăt fārms

This is clearly an iambic (˘ ‾) pentameter (five feet per line), probably the most popular metrical form in English poetry. Note that the division of a line into feet does not have to be based on *words*, but is based rather on *syllables* – the foot division, quite correctly, cuts through the middle of the word 'grazes' above.

Thōŭgh thy̆/slūmbĕr/māy bĕ/deēp,

Yĕt thy̆/spīrĭt/shāll nŏt/sleēp

Basically this is a trochaic trimeter, with an extra stressed syllable at the end of each line.

Eārth, rĕ/ceīve ăn/hōnoŭred/gŭest

Wīlliăm/Yeāts ĭs/laīd tŏ/rĕst

An example of the same metrical pattern.

Seāsŏn ŏf/mīsts ănd/mēllŏw/fruītfŭlnĕss!

Clōse bŏsŏm/-friĕnd ŏf/thĕ/matūrĭng/sūn;

A tetrameter with a mixture of trochaic and dactylic feet; note how frequently an extra stressed or unstressed syllable has to be included in poetry, as in the second lines both above and below:

Jŭst fŏr ă/hāndfŭl ŏf/sīlvĕr hĕ/lĕft ŭs,

Jŭst fŏr ă/rībănd tŏ/stīck ĭn/hĭs/coāt –

The above is another predominantly dactylic metre, in this case a tetrameter.

Ŏh, hĕ flīes/thrŏugh thĕ aīr/wĭth thĕ greā/tĕst ŏf eāse

Thĕ dār/ĭng yŏung mān/ŏn thĕ flȳ/ĭng trăpeēze

This is an anapaestic tetrameter.

Text-books quite frequently quote the poem by Samuel Taylor Coleridge (1772–1834) which illustrates five metrical patterns:

Trōchĕe trīps frŏm lōng tŏ shōrt.

Frŏm lōng tŏ lōng ĭn sōlĕmn sōrt

Slōw Spōndēe stālks; strōng fōot! yĕt ĭll āblĕ

Ēvĕr tŏ cōme ŭp wĭth Dāctўl trĭsўllăblĕ.

Ĭāmbĭcs mārch frŏm shōrt tŏ lōng.

Wĭth ă lēap ănd ă bōund thĕ swĭft Ānăpaĕsts thrōng.

This poem is useful because it also gives some insight into the different moods that metre can create. It is helpful to remember that the pronunciation of the metrical terms themselves follows their metre:

Ĭāmb, Trōchĕe, Ănăpaĕst, Dāctўl(ĭc), Spōndēe

or at least can be made to do so with only a little cheating.

Remember when you have gone to all the effort of learning how to scan a poem it is not always necessary to use the knowledge you have gained. Very few poets stick to a metre with absolute regularity. What is interesting is when the poet departs from that metre, because this is often where he has some special effect in mind.

Rhyme

Young people often think that a poem is simply something that rhymes, which is no nearer the truth than saying a poem is something with a metre. Poetry without any formal metre is called *free verse*, and poetry without any rhyme but with a metrical structure is called *blank verse*.

Rhyme is the repetition of certain sounds, at regular intervals, and usually at the ends of lines of poetry. There are various types of rhyme:

masculine rhyme: rhyme of one syllable, as in:
    boat/coat, fast/last, will/kill, sad/bad, sag/bag.
feminine/double rhyme: rhyme of two syllables, with the second syllable being unstressed, as in:
    wilful/skilful, stranger/danger, master/plaster.
triple rhyme: rhyme of a stressed syllable followed by two unstressed ones, as in:
    laborious/victorious, sufficiency/deficiency.
internal/middle rhyme: as the name suggests, this is where a poem rhymes in the middle of a line, rather than in the usual position at the end.

> *pararhyme/half-rhyme*: rhyme where the first and last consonant
> sounds are the same, but the intervening vowel is different, as in:
> flip/flop, ship/shape, leaves/lives, grained/groined.
> The technique was made famous by the poet Wilfred Owen
> (1893–1918).
> *eye rhyme*: rhyme where two words look alike, but do not sound the
> same, as in:
> bough/rough, love/move, low/how.

There are various other definitions of rhymes; the above is a basic list
sufficient for most needs, and even then all that is usually required is for
the student to know that a poem does rhyme. Rhyme is pleasing to the
ear, or should be if handled well. It can emphasise certain words, and
also reinforce a metrical pattern. It can give a ritualistic, almost mystic
tone to poetry, or simply be a unifying factor that links up lines in an
otherwise rambling structure.

The system of rhyme within any individual poem is called a 'rhyme
scheme'. The traditional way of marking down a rhyme scheme is to give
each rhyming sound (at the end of the lines) a letter of the alphabet. The
following extract from 'Auguries of Innocence' by William Blake
(1757–1827) provides a good example:

The Harlot's cry from Street to Street	*a*
Shall weave Old England's winding Sheet.	*a*
The Winner's Shout, the Loser's Curse,	*b*
Dance before dead England's Hearse.	*b*
Every Night & every Morn	*c*
Some to Misery are Born.	*c*
Every Morn & every Night	*d*
Some are Born to sweet Delight.	*d*
Some are Born to sweet Delight	*d*
Some are Born to Endless Night.	*d*

The rhyme scheme for this piece would be written, therefore, *aabb
ccdddd*.

Diction

A poet's diction is his choice of words, or the vocabulary he uses. In
theory it applies to poets, dramatists, and novelists; in practice the word
is used almost exclusively of poets. Diction can be archaic (use of old-
fashioned words, or words no longer in common use), colloquial (like
everyday speech), refined, elegant, technical, scientific, or any number
of things. At one extreme there is the colloquial diction of 'Goodbye, old
lad! Remember me to God', at the other the exalted diction of 'Avenge,

O Lord, they slaughter'd saints, whose bones/Lie scatter'd on the Alpine mountains cold'. Only mention diction when you are actually aware that a poet is using a notable diction. A remark such as 'The poet's diction is normal' gains very few marks.

General points on technique

An author uses imagery, metre, rhyme, and diction either to help create a certain sound, or to convey a certain message or impression. Beware that when you do become familiar with the various techniques of poetry you do not let your essays or your thinking become dominated by them, and end up telling the reader every technique that the poet has used, but never actually getting round to saying what all the techniques have been used *for* – what the aim of the poem is.

Try to be as aware of rhythm as you are of metre. Rhythm is less formal than metre, and many modern poets will not use formal metre. They will be aware of rhythm as a means of conveying a host of impressions, and rhythm can be as powerful an aid to a poet as metre. Try to see if a poet is using particular rhythms to evoke a mood or give a particular tone to a poem.

Literary terms

alliteration: close repetition of consonant sounds at the beginning of words, as in 'From the field of his fame fresh and gory', or 'And their sentinel stars set their watch in the sky'. ANGLO-SAXON VERSE was based on alliteration rather than rhyme.

amphibrach: a metrical foot consisting of one unstressed foot, followed by one stressed foot and a further unstressed foot.

anapaest: a metrical foot consisting of two unstressed feet followed by a stressed foot.

Anglo-Saxon verse: the Anglo-Saxon period is usually taken to mean the period between the Romans leaving Britain and the conquest of England by William of Normandy, roughly AD400–1066. Anglo-Saxon literature is the term used to describe literature of this period, although comparatively little poetry of the period survives.

assonance: close repetition of vowel sounds, usually as the stressed syllables in a line of verse, as in 'Half my love, or half my hate'.

ballad: a ballad is a narrative poem designed originally to be sung. In traditional form it is heavily biased towards action, makes use of dialogue but little characterisation, employs a simple rhyme and jog-trot rhythm or metre, and frequently employs the use of a refrain. The story is simple, often heroic or tragic, and told with great economy; supernatural events frequently take place in the course of the action.

The original traditional ballad form has been imitated by poets with great frequency. *The Ballad of Chevy Chase* and *Sir Patrick Spens* (both written anonymously and current by the fifteenth century) are two of the best-known examples of the traditional ballad. Of modern literary ballads (poems written in imitation of the ballad form but with a known author), *The Rime of the Ancient Mariner* (1798) by Samuel Taylor Coleridge (1772–1834) and 'La Belle Dame sans Merci' (1819) by John Keats (1795–1821) are probably the best-known.

blank verse: unrhymed poetry; strictly speaking, blank verse should consist of unrhymed iambic pentameters.

caesura: a pause in a line of verse, often brought in to achieve a degree of variety in a metrical or rhythmical line. The position of the caesura is often marked by punctuation, but need not be; sometimes the natural rhythms of language dictate a pause without the necessity of punctuation.

conceit: an elaborate, extended, and startling comparison between apparently dissimilar objects, associated in particular with META-PHYSICAL POETRY. When in his poem 'The Flea' the poet John Donne (1572–1631) compares his lover and himself to a flea (the flea has sucked the blood of both, and is therefore a symbol of their unity) he is composing a text-book conceit: unexpected, carried out at considerable length, and ultimately both convincing and intriguing.

couplet: a two-line section of a poem. See SHAKESPEARIAN SONNET.

courtly love: a philosophy of love and an attitude towards it that feature in the work of Geoffrey Chaucer (?1345–1400). It became formalised in the royal courts of the South of France in the twelfth century, and came to have recognised features. It dealt with aristocratic love of an extra-marital nature. The male lover was in total subservience to his mistress or lady love, and venerated her almost as a goddess. The courtly love romance was always secret. In Chaucerian or early courtly love, this love is sensual and sexual, though always treated with dignity and decorum except when the convention is being satirised (as in Chaucer's *The Merchant's Tale*); in later variations of the convention the love becomes more refined and spiritual.

Sociologists have commented that courtly love provided a counterbalance to medieval marriage, where the male held complete dominance. By the time Chaucer came to use the convention, it had moved towards a middle-class morality, and attempted to combine the extra-marital nature of the love relationship with a more conventionally acceptable marriage relationship. Thus in Chaucer's *The Franklin's Tale* the lovers have a relationship with many of the features of a courtly love romance, but are also married. This produces considerable awkwardness, and when the plot reaches a climax all pretence that the woman is dominant vanishes and the relationship returns to the conventional, male-dominated medieval marriage.

dactyl: a metrical foot consisting of one stressed and two unstressed syllables.

diction: an author's choice and use of words; his vocabulary.

dimeter: a unit of metre consisting of two feet.

dirge: a mourning poem, or song of lament, composed in commemoration of the dead. One of the best-known is the song in Shakespeare's *The Tempest* sung by Ariel of Ferdinand's lost father, beginning 'Full fathom five thy father lies;/Of his bones are coral made' (this is also an excellent example of ALLITERATION).

doggerel: crudely written, unsophisticated, rough poetry.

dramatic monologue: a poem written as if spoken aloud by one character, who in speaking reveals his personality as well as commenting on a situation. One of the best dramatic monologues in English is 'The Old Huntsman' (1917) by Siegfried Sassoon (1886–1967).

elegy: originally in Greek and Roman literature an elegy was any poem using the elegiac couplet (a dactylic hexameter followed by a dactylic pentameter or hexameter). In more recent times the term has come to mean a poem mourning the death of an individual, or of all men. A pastoral elegy has the same subject matter, but it is set in the classical pastoral world, with shepherds and goatherds as the characters. 'Elegy in a Country Churchyard' (1750) by Thomas Gray (1716–71) is one of the most famous elegies ever written; probably the best-known pastoral elegy is *Lycidas* (1637) by John Milton (1608–74).

enjambement: where one line in a poem is 'run on' into the next by an absence of any punctuation at the end of the first line.

epic: an extended narrative poem, with a heroic subject matter and theme, and an exalted tone. There are primary epics, such as the *Iliad* by Homer (*c*.ninth century BC), later literary epics such as the *Aeneid* by Virgil (70–19BC), and 'modern' epics such as *The Divine Comedy* (1320) by Dante (1265–1321) and *Paradise Lost* (1667) by Milton. The true epic starts *in medias res* (in the middle of the action), after a grand announcement of theme and an appeal to a muse; the noble hero performs many deeds of courage, there are great battles, and the characters have long set speeches in which they tell of themselves. Modern epics differ in a number of ways from the classical antecedents.

epic simile: sometimes known as a Homeric simile, this is an extended and elaborate simile. Milton's description of Satan in *Paradise Lost* extends to sixteen lines or so, the simile being to compare Satan to a whale or sea monster.

epistle: a letter; verse or poetry in the form of a letter.

epitaph: originally a verse inscription on a tombstone, now any poem which expresses a feeling for someone who is dead, usually in an attempt to sum up their lives. Despite the subject matter, many epitaphs have a comic element.

exemplum: a story told to illustrate a moral point, an 'example' of morality in action and practice.

eye rhyme: rhyme based on words that look similar but which are pronounced differently, as in how/bow (with 'bow' as in 'bow and arrow').

foot: a group of syllables forming a metrical unit.

free verse: poetry without regular metre or line length.

Georgian poetry: a group of poets popular in Britain in the early part of the twentieth century, based round the five *Georgian Poetry* anthologies published under the editorship of Edward Marsh between 1912 and 1923. The Georgians stood for greater realism in poetry, emphasis on subjective experience, and the direct expression of emotion. Originally thought of as merely a decadent last spasm of the ROMANTIC movement, they are increasingly coming to be seen as a final flowering of this movement. Authors given space in the Georgian anthologies included Rupert Brooke (1887–1915), John Masefield (1878–1967), D. H. Lawrence (1885–1930), Walter de la Mare (1873–1956), Edmund Blunden (1896–1974), and Isaac Rosenberg (1890–1918).

georgic: a poem about rustic life.

half-rhyme: rhyming of first and last consonants, with a different vowel sound in the middle, as in flip/flap, sown/sign.

heptameter: a line of verse with seven feet in it.

heroic couplet: a pair of rhymed iambic pentameters, used most skilfully by the poet Alexander Pope (1688–1744).

hexameter: a line of six metrical feet.

Horatian ode: see ODE.

iamb(us): a foot of verse consisting of one unstressed syllable followed by a stressed syllable. This is probably the most common foot in English poetry.

identical rhyme: not really rhyme at all, but the use of identical words at the end of two or more lines of poetry or verse.

Imagism: a school of poetry that flourished between 1909 and 1917 in England, and often thought of as being in opposition to the GEORGIAN poets. Imagists believed that poetry should use ordinary language, be innovative as regards technique, be free to deal with any subject, and work through hard, precise, clear imagery rather than through allowing the author's own voice to intrude into the poem. They were in part a reaction (as, ironically, were the Georgians) against the loose, sentimental, and highly subjective poetry of the latter part of the nineteenth century. Their leader and most famous champion was Ezra Pound (1885–1972).

internal rhyme: rhyme within a line, rather than at the end of it.

lament: a poem expressing intense grief.

lyric: originally a song performed to the music of the lyre, an early stringed instrument; it can now mean a song-like poem, but in general it means a fairly short poem dealing with the thoughts and feelings of a single speaker, usually, though not always, taken to be the poet.

Metaphysical poetry: the Metaphysical poets were a diverse group of poets writing between, roughly, 1610 and 1680. Metaphysical poetry (the term was invented considerably after the group flourished) is both intellectual and emotional, exploring both intellectual matters and emotional or psychological ones, usually at a high pitch of intensity. It uses ordinary speech as well as terms drawn from the science of the day (and scientific concepts also). Technical devices associated with the school are paradox (see p. 29) and CONCEIT. Love and religion were probably its most common themes and subject matter; these twin subjects were sometimes treated in the same style, with an address to a lover being phrased in the language of an address to God, and an address to God being phrased in the language and style of the romantic love poem. Authors generally held to belong to the school are John Donne (?1571–1631), Andrew Marvell (1621–78), George Herbert (1593–1633), Henry Vaughan (1622–95), John Cleveland (1613–58), Abraham Cowley (1618–67), and Richard Crashaw (?1612–49).

metre: the regular and repetitive pattern of stresses in poetry.

Miltonic sonnet: a form of SONNET introduced by the poet John Milton which has the rhyme scheme *abbaabba cdcdcd*, but which has no change or turn of meaning in the second half.

monody: a poem of mourning presented by one person.

monometer: a line of verse with one foot in it.

occasional verse: poetry written to commemorate a specific event.

octameter: a line of poetry with eight feet in it; rarely used.

octave: the first, eight-line section of a PETRARCHAN SONNET. Octave can also mean an eight-line poem.

ode: a serious poem with an elevated, dignified style, usually of some length. In an Horatian ode each STANZA follows the same metrical pattern; the best-known examples are 'Ode to a Nightingale' (?1819) by John Keats; and 'An Horatian Ode Upon Cromwell's Return From Ireland' (1650) by Andrew Marvell, which is also a good example of OCCASIONAL VERSE and METAPHYSICAL POETRY. Odes of any sort usually rhyme.

***ottava rima*:** a STANZA of eight lines in iambic pentameters rhyming *abababcc*. Well-known examples are *Don Juan* (1820) by Lord Byron

(1788–1824) and 'Sailing to Byzantium' by William Butler Yeats (1865–1939).

pentameter: a line of poetry consisting of five feet.

Petrarchan sonnet: a fourteen-line poem divided into two parts, an eight-line OCTAVE and a six-line SESTET. The octave usually rhymes *abbaabba*, the sestet *cdecde*. The octave generally states the theme, the sestet its answer or resolution. The rhyme schemes are the least binding element, and can be varied.

prosody: the theory of poetry, prosody deals with matters such as metre, rhyme, diction, and stanza patterns.

quatrain: a four-line section of a poem. See SHAKESPEARIAN SONNET.

refrain: what to non-literary students is often known as the chorus – a line or lines repeated at regular intervals, most often at the end of a STANZA.

rhyme: the use of words with similar sounds in poetry, usually but not always at the ends of lines.

Romantic poetry: Romanticism is one of the most complex terms in all literature, so much so that no exact definition exists. Romantic poetry, at least as far as English literature is concerned, is marginally easier to define, but even then the group commonly known as Romantic poets contains authors who are extremely dissimilar. The beginning of Romantic poetry is usually identified with the publication of *Lyrical Ballads* (1798, 1800, 1803) by William Wordsworth (1770–1850) and Samuel Taylor Coleridge, and as a movement in poetry it was not replaced until the 1920s; indeed it still exists in the work of a number of poets. The Romantic poet believes in the imagination and the emotions, rather than in reason. He believes in the individual, rather than in man as a social animal, and in the cultivation and revelation of the individual soul; self-analysis is a strong feature of Romantic poetry. Man is seen as naturally good, but corrupted by civilisation. The Romantic poet can be a political revolutionary, but also very often has a high regard for Nature and the natural environment, seeing in it unspoilt beauty and the basic truths that underlie all human existence. He is often searching for a transcendental moment of insight, the sublime and wonderful experience that makes life worthwhile. Romantic poets include Percy Bysshe Shelley (1792–1822), Robert Browning (1812–89), Alfred Lord Tennyson (1809–92), as well as Wordsworth, Coleridge, and Byron.

scansion: the analysis of metrical patterns in poetry.

sestet: the second, six-line section of a PETRARCHAN SONNET; it can also mean a six-line poem.

Shakespearian sonnet: a poem of fourteen lines with a metrical pattern of iambic pentameters. It has a variable rhyme scheme, and is divided into three QUATRAINS, with a concluding COUPLET; this final couplet usually expresses the theme of the poem. The great exponent of the genre is, obviously enough, Shakespeare.

sonnet: a poem of fourteen lines, with many variations of rhyme scheme and structure. There is usually a strong relationship between the form of a sonnet and its content: a sonnet divided into an OCTAVE and a SESTET, for example, may show a significant change of mood or emphasis as the poem passes from one part to the next. See MILTONIC, PETRARCHAN, SHAKESPEARIAN and SPENSERIAN SONNET.

Spenserian sonnet: a sonnet with the rhyme scheme *ababbcbccdcdee* and no break between the OCTAVE and the SESTET. Named after the poet Edmund Spenser (?1552–99).

spondee: a metrical foot containing two stressed syllables.

stanza: a group of lines in a poem divided off from the others. Each division or stanza is usually the same number of lines in length. A stanza refers to what in normal speech is often wrongly called a 'verse' of a poem. As critics talk about verse rather than poetry, a new term, stanza, is necessary. Never refer to a unit of lines in a poem as a verse; always call it a stanza.

tetrameter: a metrical unit of four feet to the line.

trimeter: a line of verse with three feet in it.

trochee: a verse foot of two syllables, the first stressed, the second unstressed.

verse: poetry; see STANZA for an explanation of its correct usage.

War Poets: the name given to the British poets of the First World War (1914–18), such as Wilfred Owen (1893–1918), Siegfried Sassoon, Isaac Rosenberg, and Edward Thomas (1878–1917).

History and reading list

Group 1: Chaucer

Pre-Chaucerian literature is usually the concern of a University department of English Literature, rather than 'O' or 'A' level students. English Literature as such starts with Chaucer (?1345–1400), if only because Chaucer was the first author to write in what was a recognisable English language. The British Isles had been subject to races using Celtic, Latin, Anglo-Saxon, Norse, and Norman French, and it was not until Chaucer's time that English as a language began to emerge. It is possible that Chaucer's works actually speeded up the formation of the independent language of English.

Chaucer was the son of prosperous upper middle-class parents, fought in France, acted as a courtier, went on diplomatic missions abroad, and eventually became Controller of Customs in London. In common with all authors of his time, his poetry was written for his own personal pleasure and that of a group of friends, with no thought of publication, which in any event was not then technically possible; writing and the study of literature was merely an accepted hobby and accomplishment for those at Chaucer's level of society. Chaucer's writings fall into three periods – the French period (1359–72), including 'The Boke of the Duchesse' (1369) and parts of 'The Romaunt of the Rose' (?1370), the Italian period (1372–86), including 'The House of Fame', 'The Parlement of Fowles', 'Troylus and Cryseyde', and 'The Legend of Good Women', and his mature period (1386–1400), from which *The Canterbury Tales* date (?1387-onwards). Of Chaucer's works *The Canterbury Tales* are by far and away the best-known.

The central concept of *The Canterbury Tales* is of a group of pilgrims travelling together for security from London to the shrine of Saint Thomas à Becket in Canterbury, in the south of England. To pass the time on their journey each pilgrim will tell two stories on the way out and two on the way back; a vote will decide who has told the best story, and he or she will be given a banquet by the other pilgrims at their expense. Chaucer states there are twenty-nine pilgrims, but he actually introduces thirty-one, including himself. The tales are also unfinished, there being only twenty-three tales in all. From this it might be deduced that the book was never completed. Chaucer uses the heroic couplet throughout the work, except for the tales where prose is used. The tales are a magnificent panorama of medieval society, missing only members of the very top level of society (who would mount their own private pilgrimages) and the very bottom (who would not be able to afford it, or gain release from their overlords).

Several of the tales feature COURTLY LOVE (see section on 'Literary Terms' above), and a number of others debate the issue of marriage, although critical opinion is divided as to whether or not there is an actual 'marriage group' of tales within the book. As each tale is told by a specific character, there is ample opportunity for comment on the teller of the tale by means of the story which he tells, and also for Chaucer's immensely skilful use of irony. Despite the difficulty of the language (diminished a great deal by the availability of excellent modern editions of the tales) Chaucer's insight and humour are as strong now as they were nearly seven hundred years ago. A major feature of his writing in *The Canterbury Tales* is the variety of his style, from the chivalric elegance of *The Knight's Tale* to the low comedy of *The Miller's Tale*.

Reading list
TEXTS:
The General Prologue
The Knight's Tale

The Miller's Tale
The Franklin's Tale

The most common examination texts, in addition to the above, include *The Merchant's Tale, The Wife of Bath's Prologue and Tale*, and *The Pardoner's Tale*.

CRITICISM:
M. W. Grose, *Chaucer* (Literature in Perspective Series).

Group 2: The Metaphysical poets

There is a considerable gap between Chaucer and the Metaphysical poets. It should not be thought that no poetry was being written during that time, rather that what poetry there was is usually not set on examination syllabuses. Sir Thomas Wyatt (1503-42) and Henry Howard, Earl of Surrey (1517-47) were both major poetic talents, specialising, as did Shakespeare, in the SONNET form (see 'Literary Terms' above). Edmund Spenser (1552-99) is another major talent, though little read in modern times except by professional critics. His major works are *The Shepherds' Calendar* (1579) and *The Faerie Queen* (1590). For a general discussion of the term METAPHYSICAL POETRY see 'Literary Terms' above. Among the individual authors John Donne (?1571-1631) still commands the most attention.

Educated as a Roman Catholic by prosperous parents, Donne became a protestant. He brought his fortunes to the lowest possible ebb by marrying Anne Moore, a niece of his patron's wife. This so angered his patron, Sir Thomas Egerton, that he had Donne imprisoned, and removed him from his job. Their dispute was later patched up, but not before Donne had spent years living on the generosity of his friends. The King, James I, considered Donne would make a good clergyman, and bowing to this pressure Donne became an Anglican priest in 1615, achieving great success, particularly as a preacher of sermons. Most of Donne's poetry was not published until after his death. It ranges from fervent love poetry, frequently of a highly sensual nature, to remarkably powerful religious poetry. The tone of all his poems is passionate and intellectual. There is a heavily dramatic quality in all his verse, and sometimes a rough energy that seems only just under control. In almost every poem he wrote Donne appears to be looking for an all-embracing mental and physical experience, a moment of total involvement and power; in some poems this is seen to be gained from love, in later poems from God and religion. In common with many authors of his and later ages he led an extremely varied life, ranging from soldier to courtier, from diplomat to clergyman. This variety is also reflected in his poems, from the deep melancholy of 'A Nocturnall upon S. Lucies Day' to the colloquial, brusque argument of 'The Sunne Rising'. Of all features it is probably the argument that stands out most forcibly from Donne's work, combining as it does the twin peaks of metaphysical poetry, passion and intellect, in the one form.

Andrew Marvell (1621–78) was hardly a contemporary of Donne's, but is undeniably a Metaphysical poet. In the words of one critic he 'manages to combine passion with formality, lightness of touch with seriousness, and lyric beauty with intelligence of argument'. There is an intellectual seriousness in most of Marvell's work which renders him quieter than Donne and less dramatic, but there is also a firmness of tone and elegance that is sometimes absent from Donne's work. Marvell is less reliant on technique than Donne, in the sense that Donne's poems occasionally rely too heavily on sweeping conceits and paradoxes. In his own time Marvell was best known as a writer and politician in favour of freedom of worship, a champion of liberty, and a powerful writer of prose pamphlets. He took a neutral position during the English Civil War, then became a supporter of Oliver Cromwell, but was allowed to retain his position under the restoration rule of Charles II.

George Herbert (1593–1633) was another poet who led an interesting life; apparently headed for an extremely successful secular career, Herbert suddenly changed tack and became a parish priest renowned for his piety and godliness. His poems were published after his death, and are highly original and individual attempts to deal with conventional issues of Christianity. There can be no doubting Herbert's fervent belief in God after a reading of his poems, but not the least of his achievements is to make this belief clear and real even to non-believers, and also to portray anguish and doubt with honesty and conviction.

Of the remaining poets Henry Vaughan (1622–95) is the one who appears most often for examination purposes. An extremely competent religious poet with the metaphysical virtues of intensity, clarity, and colloquial language, his poems tend to 'peak' at the start, and do not always quite live up to expectations.

Reading list
TEXTS:
Donne, 'Holy Sonnets'
  'The Sunne Rising'
  'A Nocturnall upon S. Lucies Day'
  'Song: Goe, and catche a falling starre'
  'The Flea'
  'Twickenham Garden'
Marvell, 'To his Coy Mistress'
  'An Horatian Ode upon Cromwell's Return from Ireland'
  'The Mower to the Glow-Worms'

'Upon Appleton House'
'The Garden'
Vaughan, 'The World'

CRITICISM:
Joan Bennett, *Five Metaphysical Poets.*

Group 3: Milton

John Milton (1608–74) is a poet who arouses strong feelings. Hailed by some as one of the major English poets of all time, by others as a fatal influence on the development of English poetry, Milton's reputation has survived in at least the minds of some examining boards. Educated at Cambridge, he appears to have taken the decision to be a poet at an early age. To a certain extent political events (the English Civil War) intervened in this ambition, for under the reign of Oliver Cromwell Milton turned his literary talents to political and religious pamphlets, and became a major writer in this mode. He was extremely fortunate to survive the Restoration of Charles II, because he had appeared to have at least a degree of sympathy with those who had ordered the execution of Charles I; other writers, including Andrew Marvell, the Metaphysical poet, interceded on his behalf, and as a result he was able to live a retired life as a poet. Married three times, the first time most unhappily, Milton went blind in his later years. His masque *Comus* (1634) has been referred to already (see p. 39); *Samson Agonistes* (1671) is another well-known poem; but it is his epic poem of the Fall of Man according to Christian doctrine, *Paradise Lost* (1674), that is Milton's major claim to fame.

Paradise Lost is perhaps the only complete successful epic in English poetry. It has its weaknesses: the characterisation of God and some of the angels is perilously heavy-handed and humourless at times, and there are distinct 'flat' passages in the poem, as well as a mildly ludicrous battle in Heaven where God fights Satan and the one-third of his angels who are in rebellion. Some critics have stated that the real hero of the poem is Satan, who, evil though he is, has courage and character in plenty. Others see Adam, prototype man, as being the real hero. Milton's language is stylised, artificial, and influenced by Latin models which can make it ponderous; but it can also be extremely powerful, evocative, and moving, with considerable flexibility and a capacity for the description of effects and incidents on the grand scale that very few other poets can match.

Reading list
TEXTS:
Paradise Lost, Books I and II
Samson Agonistes

CRITICISM:
A. J. A. Waldock, *Paradise Lost and Its Critics*.
C. Ricks, *Milton's Grand Style*.

Group 4: Alexander Pope and the eighteenth century

The eighteenth century produced one of England's major poetic talents, Alexander Pope (1688–1744), a man who has in his way become a symbol for the 'Augustan' age of poetry – that is, an age of literary brilliance that was considered comparable to Rome under Emperor Augustus (27BC–AD14) when Virgil, Horace and Ovid flourished. Pope was a Roman Catholic, and as a result of childhood illness lived his life with a deformed spine. His first major work was his *Essay on Criticism* (1711), followed by the famous MOCK HEROIC (see p. 28) poem *The Rape of the Lock* (1712–14). Pope then translated two of the great classical epic poems, the *Iliad* and the *Odyssey* of Homer (these translations appeared in 1715–20 and 1725–6 respectively). Pope's aim in translating these poems was to bring these great works within reach of ordinary literate people, but they had another distinct advantage for Pope: they allowed him to become almost the first 'professional' writer, in the sense of a non-dramatic author who earned all his income from his writing and its sales. Previously poets had needed a rich patron to finance their writing. Pope followed the opening sections of the *Iliad* with *Eloisa to Abelard* (1717), the *Dunciad* (1728), *Epistle to Dr Arbuthnot* (1735), and the *Essay on Man* (1734).

Pope's writings marked a new style and approach to poetry, and one which has become associated with the eighteenth century. He wrote in HEROIC COUPLETS (see 'Literary Terms' above), in a manner that was often critical of society. Satire was Pope's favourite medium, aimed against individuals and against the society which produced them. He had a deep moral concern, and saw the poet as someone part of whose task was to keep society healthy and to purge it of its sickness by the medium of satire. Pope was a hugely passionate man, but the passion is not the same as that of the Metaphysical poets, or Shakespeare. It is more formal, more social, and even more elegant: a deftly-wielded razor-sharp rapier of passion directed largely against human weakness, although it does also convey an awareness of human strengths. Just as Chaucer saw his characters partly as what they were, and partly as what they contributed to society as a whole, so Pope's concern is similarly social. The strength of Pope's passion and convictions made him a number of enemies, enemies whose attacks did not stop short of physical, cruel abuse directed at his physical disabilities. The bitterness he felt at these attacks is visible in his work, but so also is his vision of man as a social animal, to be judged in the final count on his contribution to society as a whole.

Pope is less influential than is sometimes supposed, but the virtues and the vices of his poetry can stand, to quite a large extent, for those of his century. The early Elizabethan period had been one of huge optimism and growth, entering a slow decline during the latter part of Elizabeth's reign and the opening of James I's. A self-questioning violence in literature follows this change. Milton reflected the growth of Puritan, Protestant confidence, the Restoration dramatists a sudden release of passion, excitement, and vitality. It was in the eighteenth century that the seeds of modern western European society began to be sown, socially and economically, and this new-found confidence and belief in progress can be seen in Pope's work perhaps more than in the work of any of his contemporaries. Oddly perhaps for an age that looked forward, its literature very often looked back to classical models, as is witnessed by Pope's labours with the *Iliad* and the *Odyssey*. From the Restoration period right up to the last decades of the eighteenth century classical models began to exert a grip on literature that was eventually to prove a stranglehold, and pave the way for the new wave of authors to come to dominate the literary scene. Pope himself had the originality of talent to profit from the past; many later writers did not.

As a final comment, Pope should also be given his due in one area that is often overlooked. The heroic couplet is a rhyming technique, and no poet in the English language has made rhyme look easier or more suited to his needs than Pope, despite the notorious difficulty of English as a rhyming language.

Reading list
TEXTS:
The Rape of the Lock
Epistle to Dr Arbuthnot

CRITICISM:
J. Sutherland, *A Preface to Eighteenth-Century Poetry.*

Group 5: The Romantic poets

The eighteenth century was above all the age of reason, an age which believed in and cultivated the intellectual, rational side of man's nature as against the emotional, passionate side. The age of Pope and the age of Wordsworth typify, respectively, the Classical and Romantic ethos, but before we proceed to examine this changeover, two relatively unsung heroes demand to be mentioned, the one ushering in the age of Pope, the other ushering in the age of Wordsworth, and both sadly neglected on a number of examination syllabuses. John Dryden's play *All for Love* has already been mentioned as one of the few successful Restoration tragedies (see p. 51), but Dryden was a poet as well as a dramatist, and though his *Absalom and Achitophel* is the only one of his poems that most modern students are familiar with, his command of verse satire and the passionate elegance of his work make him a natural bridge between the Metaphysical poets and Pope. At the other end of the time scale is the remarkable William Blake (1757–1827). Put kindly, Blake was highly eccentric; put bluntly, he was mad. He had visions in which he met and talked to angels and other such spiritual creatures, and his wife was forced to place an empty plate in front of him on the frequent occasions when he had overlooked the necessity of doing some work in order to buy some food. One visitor to the Blake household found him and his wife in the garden, clothed only in an occasional leaf, reading Milton's *Paradise Lost* and by their state of undress hoping to feel closer to Adam and Eve. Blake was an engraver whose work stops short of genius only through a slightly clumsy drawing technique typical of his age. His poetic writings are vast in their quantity and their scope; he invented whole new mythologies and religions, and was a visionary writer of the utmost significance, but he is still best known for some of his earliest work, the *Songs of Innocence* and *Songs of Experience* (1789 and 1794), where innocence and experience are described with a simple purity and stark grimness respectively.

As often happens in literature, at the end of the eighteenth century the pendulum swung from one extreme to another: from reason into passion. The distinction between a 'Classical age' and a 'Romantic age' is one of the most vexed issues of literature, and what follows can only hope to scratch at the surface of the problem. It is possible to see two basically different ways of looking at life and experience, and tag these two different approaches as the Classical and the Romantic. Pope's age was, by and large, the Classical age. It believed in reason, the control of the passions and the instinct, the essential perfectibility of mankind, the steady march of progress; it believed that civilisation, as attained in Greek and Roman times, was within the grasp also of the 'modern' age. It is not difficult to see historical reasons for this attitude in the eighteenth century – perhaps it is even too easy to see the links. Reforms in medical care and farming techniques in the eighteenth century began to allow the rise in Great Britain's population that was to be a major factor in the Industrial Revolution – the process by which Great Britain became the first nation in the world to move from a farming to an industrial economy. Discoveries were beginning to be made in the sciences, engineering, and even in the social sciences that were to change the face of British society. It must have appeared that mankind was set on a new advance, and one which could only bring benefit to all. This confidence is perhaps more visible in the novel than it is in poetry. The Romantic outlook, on the other hand, sees man's salvation as lying within himself. The Romantic believes in and trusts only himself, believing that society and civilisation corrupt humanity's natural innocence and instinct for good. Romantic literature, particularly poetry, often sees man in communion with the natural world, rather than with other men; it trusts instinct, the emotions, and the heart, rather than reason and the head. The distinction is perhaps best illustrated by two specific examples. The 'noble savage' concept is specifically a Romantic one. It consists of the idea that man in his primitive state is in a higher state of purity than civilised, urban man, whose natural instincts have been ground out of him by the process of civilised life. The savage may appear primitive, but the truth is that he has an instinctive knowledge of himself and the world often superior to that which has been acquired by civilised man. The Classicist would laugh derisively at this concept. To him the savage is just what the word states – a human in a savage state of primitive bestiality whose only hope lies in his being educated and brought up the scale of evolution by application of the civilised virtues. The savage represents crude, unrefined, static man, a hopeless bundle of raw instinct and repulsive primitivism, and a denial of all capacity for progress in humanity. Only a Romantic would think of a savage as noble; to a Classicist, he would be merely sad and regrettable.

Nowhere is this better seen than in the different attitudes to children shown in the work of poets influenced by the two different outlooks. To Pope a child is important only in as much as he will become an adult, and a civilised being. As a child his instincts have yet to be trained, and he is too near the level of a savage to be a true person. Pope's attitudes are those of a Classical age, where it is the adult who is important, not the child, and childhood is merely a temporary state which is necessary before adulthood can be attained, and with it real humanity. To a Romantic, a child is in some respects a holier and purer object than an adult. The child is unspoilt by civilisation, uncorrupted, in a natural state that can even mean he is closer to God and the sources of creation than are his older fellows. Rather than being something to be hurried out of, childhood to a Romantic is a state to be envied, cultivated, and enhanced, as well as admired. If an author's work contains a picture of a child who is valued and thought highly of simply as a child, then the odds are that the author is biased towards a Romantic outlook; if on the other hand the child appears in the author's work as only worth something for the adult features he displays, and childhood appears as an irritating state to be grown out of as quickly as possible, then the chances are that the author is biased towards Classicism. We must, however, be wary in applying this test: an author such as Charles Dickens can appear to be praising children who are old before their time when he is actually damning those who make children embark on this process of early maturity. A Romantic author will usually use unkindness towards children as the ultimate damnation; a Classical author is just as likely to use unkindness against adults, and to ignore children altogether.

In general, a Classical author tends to turn his attention outward to the society in which he or she lives, whilst a Romantic exposes his own soul, directing the light of analysis and comment internally. This analysis, of course, indicates the two extremes, and most ages and types of literature share Classical and Romantic features.

William Wordsworth (1770–1850) is perhaps the best-known of all the Romantic poets. He was born in the Lake District, in Cumberland; his love of the English Lakes never left him and remained to the end a major influence in all he wrote. He was greatly excited by the French Revolution (1789), seeing in it the chance for a whole new order in the world, and while in France he fathered an illegitimate child. When the French Revolution turned towards tyranny, and England declared war on France, Wordsworth suffered intense disappointment which brought him near to mental collapse. His child and her mother were beyond his reach because of the war, and his loyalties were divided between France – the ideals of the Revolution and his love affair – and England. Guilt and confusion threatened to swallow Wordsworth up, and his sister Dorothy was a major factor in ensuring that he regained his composure. It is sometimes stated that great authors, or writers of genius, are at war with themselves. If this is so then Wordsworth must be the prime proof of the idea. In the years when he was tortured by guilt and unanswered questions he wrote the poetry by which he is remembered; he died in 1850, but wrote the vast majority of the poems on which his reputation is based by 1807.

Wordsworth launched his poetic career in collaboration with Samuel Taylor Coleridge (see below); they jointly published *Lyrical Ballads* (1798), which contained 'Tintern Abbey', one of Wordsworth's best-known poems. Wordsworth stated explicitly in the introduction to this volume that he was aiming to move poetry away from the clichés and the stylised, elaborate renderings that were popular at the time, and towards the language of everyday speech and the experience of common people, at the same time showing man in relation to his natural environment. In doing this some poems in the *Lyrical Ballads* are so base and common as to be unintentionally funny, but others have considerable power. An altogether more effective explanation of Wordsworth's poetic philosophy is found in the Preface to the 1800 edition of the *Lyrical Ballads*.

Perhaps Wordsworth's major work was *The Prelude*, started in 1799 and completed in 1805, but not published until after his death, in 1850. This is a lengthy autobiographical poem of mixed merit: some of the linking sections demonstrate Wordsworth's inability to throw away anything he wrote even if it deserves it, but other sections show him at his most powerful. It is a sad comment on his declining inspiration that most editors print two versions of *The Prelude*, the original and the revised version, or simply leave out the revised, later version, in which the poet working in his maturity manages to undo many of the main achievements of the early version.

Wordsworth excels at taking one particular moment of experience and conveying it richly and effectively with a hint of moral comment that enlarges the reader's perception of what is taking place and gives it significance without swamping him. As a nature poet and a poet willing and able to see man against a backdrop of nature he has no equal.

John Keats (1795–1821) was another major poetic talent, and, as is the case with many of the Romantic poets, very different in style and approach from Wordsworth. He is best known for his odes, in particular 'Ode to a Nightingale' (1820), 'Ode on a Grecian Urn' (1820), 'Ode to Melancholy' (?1820), 'Ode to Autumn' (?1820). These odes have the verbal luxuriance and almost sensual evocation of mood that are often associated with Romantic poetry; they also have a sharpness of intellectual enquiry and a residual Classicism in the imagery that is entirely Keats's own. The control and tightness displayed in the odes appears to elude Keats in some of his longer poems. One of his great concerns was the nature and meaning of art, a topic covered extensively in the odes, and also in his magnificent letters, most of which were published after his death.

Samuel Taylor Coleridge (1772–1834) was a close friend and associate of Wordsworth. He was and is a perplexing personality – an opium addict also partly addicted to self-pity, a brilliant conversationalist and a personality capable of inspiring the warmest feelings of friendship, a poet of the highest imaginative power who somehow never quite lives up to his promise except in a few of his poems. Coleridge is best known for *The Rime of the Ancient Mariner*, published in *Lyrical Ballads*, a poem with an imaginative power and strangeness that brings it close to MYTH (see p. 28–9). The poem is simple, stark, nightmarish; it has a raw energy and a unique flavour to it that no other author has equalled since, and for all its self-evident power there has been no convincing explanation as to why its symbolism is at one and the same time so demonstrably effective and yet so ambiguous. 'Kubla Khan', the product of an interrupted opium dream, is also well known and an highly effective poem.

Lord Byron (1788–1824) was an even more dramatic figure than Coleridge. Wild, extravagant, unconventional, tormented and torment-ing, Byron is perhaps the most Romantic of the Romantics. He was accused of most things during his lifetime, including an undeniable sexual relationship with his half-sister. *Don Juan* (1819–24) is the work on which his modern reputation is largely based. It is humorous, satirical, daring, shrewd, and moving at varying times, but the predominant tone is one of elegant and sophisticated irony, enlivened by the occasional huge incongruity. *Childe Harold* (1812–18), an earlier work, shows many of the same features of *Don Juan*, albeit in less mature form, and is also autobiographical. Byron was a tormented figure, a devil perhaps, but a devil who could see the ironies of his own behaviour, and who had perhaps chosen devildom because, in the last count, no-one had offered anything more exciting.

Percy Bysshe Shelley (1792–1822) is another great name of Romantic poetry. He died much as he had lived, in a storm. His first wife committed suicide, he arranged for his own expulsion from Oxford University, and his whole life seems to have been based on change, tumult, and uncertainty. Shelley was a visionary, and a prophet. He had little or no sense of humour, and the occasionally vague and abstract quality in his work leaves certain critics uneasy. He was undoubtedly obsessed with himself, out of touch sometimes with real life, and illogical and unrealistic. He is perhaps at his best when he ceases to try and preach a moral, and sticks to creating a mood. He is best known for *Prometheus Unbound* (1820), a verse drama telling of man's redemption by love, and for several poems amongst which are 'Ode to a Skylark', and 'Ode to the West Wind' (both 1820), and 'Ozymandias' (?1821). He was a friend of Byron, and wrote a satire against Wordsworth as well as a poem mourning the death of Keats – all indications of his identity as a Romantic.

Alfred, Lord Tennyson is a late Romantic (1809–92), and a poet who was for many years extremely unfashionable, despite or even because of huge popularity in his own lifetime. Tennyson is one of a number of poets who have been partially damned with the comment that they were or are fine technicians, that is, authors well able to command the disciplines of rhyme, rhythm, and metre, but without the inspiration to bring the content of their poetry up to the standard of its form. It is certainly true that Tennyson shared with a number of other Romantic poets an inability to find the waste paper basket, and it is also true that he is not the most intellectual of poets. However, there is deep thought and feeling in his poetry, even if it is sometimes ponderous and slow, and when this is allied to an exceptional command of rhyme and rhythms it can make for a very powerful mixture. Tennyson was never able to move beyond the confines of Victorian morality and to comment objectively on his own age, and thus his poetry is sometimes strangled by a rather parochial view and outlook.

In Memoriam (1850) is a long poem composed over a number of years, its starting point being the death of Tennyson's friend Arthur Hallam. It was one of Queen Victoria's favourite poems (a fact which on its own has served to damn Tennyson in the eyes of some modern critics), and though it suffers from a lack of any real philosophical or intellectual enquiry, it does have a degree of thought and a large amount of feeling which at times flower into something wholly moving and effective. His *Idylls of the King* (1859) showed his fondness for the simple, heroic mode, and have been criticised for being legend converted to the task of Victorian moralising. The longer poems are probably not the ones that the student should turn to initially. Instead, some of his shorter lyrics and poems are extremely effective and readily graspable at first reading, such as 'The Lady of Shalott' and 'The Lotus Eaters' (1833), 'Mariana of the Moated Grange' (1830), 'Ulysses' (1842), and 'The Revenge' (1880).

Robert Browning (1812–89) came to fame late in his life, but then achieved a reputation that rivalled Tennyson's. A dramatist as well as a poet, Browning wrote his most famous poetry in the DRAMATIC MONO-LOGUE form (see 'Literary Terms' above). His main interest is the psychological complexities of human character, and thus his poems do not rely on narrative or a story so much as an exposition of a static situation or state of mind. His language lacks the luscious decorative features of some other Romantic poets, and, like Tennyson, he is a superb manipulator of rhythm and metre. He can also be very obscure, particularly in his later poetry, and makes metre and rhythm intrusive. Browning is optimistic, full of vitality, and occasionally slightly complacent. Some of his best-known poems are 'My Last Duchess' (1842), 'Andrea del Sarto' (1855), and the collection *Men and Women* (1855). As with Tennyson, his longer works, notably *The Ring and the Book* (1868–9), are generally held to be less of a success, and are certainly more difficult.

Reading list
TEXTS:
Wordsworth, *The Prelude*.
Keats, 'Odes'.
Coleridge, 'The Rime of the Ancient Mariner'.
Tennyson, 'The Lady of Shallott'
    'Mariana of the Moated Grange'.

Group 6: The War poets

As with all movements, the Romantic movement eventually degenerated, but before it did so there was one last flowering, a tragic one brought about by the First World War (1914–18). War poetry as such means simply poetry written about war, and there is no shortage of that throughout history. The term 'War Poets' has arisen because the First World War produced a distinct and unique body of poetry about that war written by young men who were for the most part born within a few years of each other, many of whom died within a few months, and even a few miles, of each other. No other war had produced a body of literature quite like this because no other war had placed so many potential poets in uniform. The demands of the battle front meant that England's professional army was not enough to fight the war, as was also the case with all the other combatant nations, and so mass conscription had to be introduced. Thus a much wider range of young men than had been normal was sucked into the war, men who were accustomed to writing poetry in something of the same way that the Elizabethan courtier had seen it as a normal part of his life. Not only were there more poets in the ranks and amongst the officers (in 1914 poetry was extremely popular), but the nature of the war itself, with the armies locked in seemingly endless conflict across a short strip of land only a few miles wide, and its peculiar horror for people unaccustomed to the brutality and waste of modern warfare, made it almost inevitable that much poetry would be written, and bearing a unique tone and flavour.

Wilfred Owen (1893–1918) held Shelley as one of his models, and had Shelley's sense of mission and his vision of the poet as prophet. Owen's early work is overladen with Romantic luxuriousness, and it was not until 1917, when he was put in hospital for nervous shock after dreadful experiences at the front, that his poetry seemed to find with a wide degree of consistency a voice and a form suitable for describing the war. His period in hospital allowed him to meet Siegfried Sassoon (see below), a more experienced poet, and shortly after this Owen began to write more in the realistic, colloquial, satirical vein of Sassoon. Owen quickly showed that he could master the styles of war poetry already in existence. His poems 'The Letter' and 'The Chances' are masterpieces of the slangy, colloquial language, and satirical style championed by Sassoon. 'Dulce et Decorum Est' is a bitter satirical poem, but also one which describes in revoltingly harsh detail the physical obscenities of the fighting. However, it is in poems such as 'Strange Meeting', 'Anthem for Doomed Youth', and 'The Send-Off' that Owen's poetry reaches its true climax. Poems such as these evoke a vast pity and sense of loss, and combine all the force of a personal complaint with the objective power of a universal statement, in which self-pity is totally removed from the poetry, and a sense of the ultimate tragedy of war for all men is evoked calmly and with great passion. Owen was a technical innovator, particularly in the area of sound in poetry. His use of ALLITERATION, ASSONANCE, and HALF-RHYME (see 'Literary Terms' above) are particularly notable.

Siegfried Sassoon (1886–1967) became famous for his bitter, satirical poems which finished on an ironic final line that threw the whole poem into relief; good examples are 'The General', 'Blighters', and 'The One-Legged Man'. Sassoon also wrote a number of poems in the DRAMATIC

MONOLOGUE form (see 'Literary Terms' above), which are perhaps underestimated by modern criticism; two fine examples are 'To Any Dead Officer' and 'Repression of War Experience'. Sassoon also wrote two extremely well-received novels, *Memoirs of a Fox-Hunting Man* (1928) and *Memoirs of an Infantry Officer* (1930), and continued to write poetry until the time of his death, but none of it had the impact of his war poetry. He is also well-known for his protest against the war which involved a letter to *The Times* newspaper and various other actions that could have given the military authorities a reason to have him shot as a traitor, even though he had been an extremely brave soldier and became known as 'Mad Jack'. He was rescued from this predicament by his friend Robert Graves, who persuaded the authorities to treat Sassoon as mentally ill, a decision which resulted in his being sent to the same hospital as Wilfred Owen.

Robert Graves (*b*.1895) himself is a major force in modern poetry. His later work has concentrated on evolving what is almost a private mythology or philosophy centred on a Muse that is both a constructive and a destructive force. His war poetry was brutal and direct, but almost all of it has been removed from editions of his *Collected Poems* by Graves himself, and it can be extremely difficult to find copies as a result of the author's hostility to his early work.

Isaac Rosenberg (1890–1918) is in some danger of becoming a cult figure, because as a Jew and the only major poet of the war who was not an officer he occupies a unique position. He was a trained artist of some distinction, though he achieved little recognition for this in his own lifetime, and invites comparison with another poor artist-poet of London, William Blake (see above). Rosenberg's poetry has a visionary fervour and power that makes it unique amongst the war poems. His form is sometimes anarchic, and he has little or no control of narrative, rhyme, or metre, but his excellence lies in symbolic imagery and the immense power of his vision, as well as in his capacity to see the war in global and cosmic terms, rather than just as a personal affront. 'Break of Day in the Trenches', 'Returning, We Hear the Larks', and 'Dead Man's Dump' are particularly fine examples of his work. An honest assessment of Rosenberg (a difficult thing to find) demands recognition of the fact that he can also be appallingly obscure and ranting. When he writes well he does so with a conviction and fire not found in any other war poet; when he writes badly, he achieves a level at the opposite extreme.

Charles Hamilton Sorley (1895–1915) had a minute output of poetry, but was remarkable for his objectivity and clarity of vision, as well as his rhythmic control. Edmund Blunden (1896–1974) was the most PASTORAL (see p. 29) of the War Poets, only altering his style and subject matter somewhat grudgingly to take account of the war, whilst Edward Thomas (1878–1917) was certainly a major poet, but wrote hardly anything that relates directly to the war. *In Parenthesis* by David Jones (1895–1974) is a long poem, written after the war, and is a mixture of prose and free verse dealing in an autobiographical manner with his experiences during the war.

Reading list
TEXTS:
Owen, 'Strange Meeting'
  'The Send-Off'
Sassoon, 'The General'
  'Blighters'
  'To Any Dead Officer'
Rosenberg, 'Break of Day in the Trenches'
  'Dead Man's Dump'

CRITICISM:
P. Fussell, *The Great War and Modern Memory*.
B. Bergonzi, *Heroes' Twilight*.
J. Stallworthy, *Wilfred Owen*.

Group 7: T. S. Eliot, W. B. Yeats and W. H. Auden

One poet who could appear as a Romantic, a War Poet, and a representative of modern poetry is Thomas Hardy (1840–1928), perhaps better known as a novelist. Hardy had the Romantic capacity to write and publish too much, and his poetry can be rhythmically awkward, mundane, and tedious; it can also be moving, observant, and innovatory. However, the modern age in poetry really begins with T. S. Eliot (1888–1965). Eliot's poetry moved from scepticism and despair to a Christian faith and hope, but it is arguably his earlier poetry which signalled the end of the Romantic movement and which made him the most influential poet of the century. *Prufrock and Other Observations* (1917) and *The Waste Land* (1922) revolutionised poetry. Late Romantic poetry had become trivial, dominated by easy pictures of nature, and riddled with cliché. Eliot used a kaleidoscope of imagery and reference to other authors and myth to present a picture of a rotten, sterile society, a corrupt and hollow shell with a past but no future. The city dominated his imagery, but he is a modern poet in more senses than this; the mood evoked in his early work reflects a society whose confidence had been shattered by global war and suffering, and which seemed to have lost purpose and direction. Eliot made poetry more difficult. The concepts he was advancing were often complex; his continual references to myths (some of them very obscure) and the work of other authors made his poetry appeal more to an educated and literate readership. There is little doubt that his poetry reflects his own comment that poetry does not have to be understood in order to communicate. *The Hollow Men* (1925) shows his movement towards Christianity, whilst *Four Quartets* (1936) is arguably his most advanced and complex work. As with all changes in fashion, Eliot's poetic revolution was complex in its effects. He did poetry a good service by rescuing it from triviality and making it an intelligent man's medium again, and the urban element in his work was a necessary and vital change for poetry; but his imitators have sometimes given their readers Eliot's obscurity without the essential vision and wisdom that underlie the original, and made a virtue out of incomprehensibility.

W. B. Yeats (1865–1939) was both a Romantic and a modern poet. An Irishman with a lasting love of and concern for his country, his early work was full of melody and decoration, luscious poetry in the Romantic or late-Romantic style; 'The Lake Isle of Innisfree' is a good example of this style. Yeats then managed that most difficult of tasks, to change with the times, and began to produce verse that was still beautiful, but also austere, refined, and lean. The change is clearly visible in *The Tower* (1928), a volume containing some of his finest poems. 'Under Ben Bulben' from *Last Poems* (1939) is Yeats's epitaph on himself, and proclaims forcibly the extent to which he saw himself as an Irish poet writing for Irishmen. His influence on the Irish theatre was immense, and his energy and commitment alone make him one of the dominant figures of twentieth-century literature. He achieved a degree of notoriety by his lack of enthusiasm for the War Poets, but the howls of protest that greeted his decision to leave out Owen, Rosenberg, and the rest of the trench poets from a popular anthology which he was editing ignored the fact that his reasons for the omission were at least based on a very viable and coherent philosophy of poetry.

Debate still rages over whether or not W. H. Auden (1907–73) is a great poet, or merely a good one. He is certainly a poet like Tennyson who can be damned by lavish praise of his technical skill, as distinct from the content of his poetry; it is also said that he 'peaked' very early, and wrote little of lasting merit after 1939. It is certainly true that he reached a high level of fame extremely early in his career, and that his latest poems appear in part to suffer from a declining inspiration. It is also true that he has written some outstanding poetry, and, though infuriatingly erratic in his achievement, that he is a major influence on modern poetry and modern poets. His early work was dominated by the burning intellectual, philosophical and political issues of post-war Europe, in particular Marxism – the theory and practice of socialism as outlined by Karl Marx (1818–1883) – and the psycho-analytical work of Sigmund Freud (1856–1939) and Carl Gustav Jung (1875–1961); like T. S. Eliot, he later converted to Christianity. But whereas Eliot became a British citizen having been born an American citizen. Auden emigrated to the United States in 1939 and eventually became an American citizen. Auden is an intellectual poet; in some respects he would be more at home in the eighteenth century than in the twentieth. He is excited by ideas as abstract concepts, and there is relatively little personal involvement in his work. The poems 'In Memory of W. B. Yeats' and 'The Shield of Achilles', from his middle period, both show his control over rhythmic forces, his intellectual insight, and the sharp clarity of his imagery.

Reading list
TEXTS:
Eliot, *The Waste Land*
Auden, 'To the Unknown Citizen'
  'In Memory of W. B. Yeats'
  'The Shield of Achilles'
Yeats, 'The Lake Isle of Innisfree'
  'Sailing to Byzantium'
  'The Second Coming'
  'Under Ben Bulben'
Hardy, 'The Convergence of the Twain'
  'The Darkling Thrush'

CRITICISM:
J. Press, *A Map of Modern English Verse.*
C. K. Stead, *The New Poetic: Yeats to Eliot.*

Group 8: Modern poetry

The term 'modern poetry' can include poetry that was written as long ago as the First World War, but in general usage the term usually implies poetry written by authors who are either still alive or who have died only recently. In the mid-1950s poetry took second place to drama, as already discussed. This did not mean that no good poetry was written, merely that in terms of trend-setting and youthful innovation drama held the lead. Poetry from the 1950s onwards has been a medium in a state of uncertainty; there have been good poets in plenty, but none who have unquestionably earned the right to be known as great, and certainly no figure comparable in significance to Wordsworth in the 1790s, or Eliot in the 1920s.

Philip Larkin (*b*.1922) is extremely well known, though it has been suggested that his warmest support comes from teachers and academics, rather from a wide readership in general. Larkin's poetry is not cheerful. It is extremely observant, both of people and of places, very often amusing albeit in a bitter, mildly cynical way, and seeks to observe rather than to alter; there is none of Shelley's or Blake's messianic, prophetic fervour in Larkin's work. It is skilfully written and presented, and perhaps in the final count just too negative to earn the title of great poetry.

Ted Hughes (b.1930) is best known for his nature poetry, in which he concentrates on the single-minded violence and forcefulness of nature, seeing man as weak in comparison, with his urge for survival diluted by his capacity for abstract thought. Hughes is forceful, compelling, direct, and occasionally criticised for a lack of subtlety.

Thom Gunn (b.1929) is thought by many to be the equal of Ted Hughes, but as a poet of abstract thought with an interest in form and a concept of violence at the heart of at least some of his poetry he has not found favour with the majority of examining boards.

A poet who, paradoxically, has also not found favour with examination boards, but for almost the opposite reason, is John Betjeman (b.1906). Betjeman has been called trivial, snobbish, and sentimental, and is perhaps too simple for most examiners, who like to give their students something to chew on, and are often wary of authors who can be wholly explained with relative ease. Betjeman's poetry is highly observant, blessed with an excellent delicacy of comic response, and more richly textured than it might sometimes appear on the surface.

Authors who are found on a majority of examination courses are R. S. Thomas (b.1913) and Seamus Heaney (b.1939). Thomas was for many years a priest working in Welsh hill-farming country. His poetry is bleak, powerful, at once a celebration of man's strength and an agonised lament at his primitivism, coupled with a religious man's soul-searching and struggle to define his relationship with God. Heaney is the modern poet who most of all succeeds through his imagery; his remembered pictures of an Irish childhood and of rural scenes have an immediacy and depth wholly due to Heaney's startling yet simple technique. Heaney is a poet of mood and moment, not a prophet who will deal with all the world's ills, but is none the worse for that.

The so-called 'Liverpool Sound' in poetry reached notoriety at roughly the same time as their fellow Liverpudlians, *The Beatles*. Irreverent, flippant, occasionally shocking, they have reached a wide audience and by the nature of what they have written, and by linking poetry with rock music, theatre, and film they have done a great deal to make poetry popular again. Leading exponents are Brian Patten (b.1946), Roger McGough (b.1937), and Adrian Henri (b.1932).

Other poets with a significant following are Donald Davie (b.1922), D. J. Enright (b.1920), Geoffrey Hill (b.1932), Laurence Lerner (b.1925), and George Macbeth (b.1932). This list is, of course, only a handful of the competent authors writing poetry today; the best method to approach modern poetry is to buy a representative anthology and make up your own mind about what you like.

Reading list
TEXTS:
A. Alvarez (ed.), *The New Poetry*.
Philip Larkin, *The Whitsun Weddings*.
Seamus Heaney, *Death of a Naturalist*.
Thom Gunn and Ted Hughes, *Selected Poems*.

CRITICISM:
Anthony Thwaite, *Poetry Today: 1960–1973*.

Practical criticism and appreciation

Rather than giving one specimen answer where the student might know the text in advance, and one where the text set is unseen, both the examples treated below are answered as if they were unseen. In fact, the technique for answering questions on unseen poetry is hardly different from the technique for answering questions on poetry you have studied, except that you are not, of course, asked to relate the poem to the work of the author as a whole.

Question 1

Write an appreciation of the poem below:

To his Coy Mistress

Had we but World enough, and Time,
This coyness Lady were no crime.
We would sit down, and think which way
To walk, and pass our long Loves Day.
Thou by the *Indian Ganges* side
Should'st Rubies find: I by the Tide
Of *Humber* would complain. I would
Love you ten years before the Flood:
And you should if you please refuse
Till the Conversion of the *Jews*.
My vegetable Love should grow
Vaster then Empires, and more slow.
An hundred years should go to praise
Thine Eyes, and on thy Forehead Gaze.
Two hundred to adore each Breast;
But thirty thousand to the rest.
An Age at least to every part,
And the last Age should show your Heart.
For Lady you deserve this State;
Nor would I love at lower rate.

But at my back I alwaies hear
Times winged Charriot hurrying near:
And yonder all before us lye
Desarts of vast Eternity.
Thy Beauty shall no more be found,
Nor, in thy marble Vault, shall sound
My ecchoing Song: then Worms shall try
That long preserv'd Virginity:
And your quaint Honour turn to dust;
And into ashes all my Lust.
The Grave's a fine and private place,
But none I think do there embrace.
Now therefore, while the youthful hew
Sits on thy skin like morning dew,
And while thy willing Soul transpires
At every pore with instant Fires,
Now let us sport us while we may;
And now, like am'rous birds of prey,
Rather at once our Time devour,
Than languish in his slow-chapt pow'r.
Let us roll all our Strength, and all
Our sweetness, up into one Ball:
And tear our Pleasures with rough strife,
Thorough the Iron gates of Life.
Thus, though we cannot make our Sun
Stand still, yet we will make him run.

Advice: Any essay needs a structure or plan for the student to work to, and some essays give what is in effect a plan by the way the title is phrased; there is no such luck with this title. Rather than just writing down an answer to this question straight away it might be worthwhile working through it in rough in the first instance.

Technique is usually a good starting point for a practical criticism of a poem, so the first step is to see if the poem is written in metre. The answer is a firm yes:

Hād wĕ/bŭt Wōrld/ĕnŏugh,/ănd Tīme,

Thĭs cōy/nĕss Lā/dў wēre/nŏ crīme

The metre is iambic, and there are four feet in each line; the poem is, therefore, written in iambic tetrameters. There are of course, variations from this, as is visible in the first line above, where a trochaic foot starts off the poem. Why? Probably to give it a dramatic start . . . or is it that the first syllable is actually unstressed, and the foot merely a standard iambic one? The only way to deal with this problem is to read the poem through and see which way reads naturally and most easily. When the metre is established you should look through the poem and see where the poet varies the metrical pattern. The opening line affords a good example. Line four ('lo̅ng Lo̅ves Da̅y') is another, the extra stress presumably being there to emphasise the heavy length of time stated in the words. A trochaic foot starts off line five, presumably for variety, and there is another in line 6. There is a spondee in line 12 ('Va̅ste̅r'), again probably to give added weight and significance to the word. A spondee and a pyrrhic foot start off line 18. Work through the rest of the poem on your own and see what other variations you can find, and then compare your answer with that given later in this section. In planning your essay, you should, therefore, first of all jot down all variations or significant points about the metre, then see if they form a pattern, and look for the major points of significance; transfer both items of information on to a note plan.

The poem has a clear *aabbcc* rhyme scheme, and so rhyme might well be the next point at which to look. Occasionally the rhyme is not exact ('would' and 'Flood'), but in general there is little sign of strain in the rhyming, which, when taken in conjunction with the regular metre, gives the poem a controlled and reflective tone, rather than the feeling of an experience being lived through then and there on the page in front of the reader. One effect of the rhyme is to give the poem a pleasant musical effect whilst at the same time making it slightly less immediate than might otherwise have been the case. The poet has given the poem a strong structure. The imagery is superficially unremarkable. The contrast between the exotic 'Ganges' and the filthy 'Humber' suggests the author has a sense of humour – as does another passage. Can you find it? In fact there are two examples of sexual humour in the poem. At this point the student may begin to feel he has exposed something in the poem. The imagery becomes more specific as the poem progresses, and the pattern follows the division of the poem into three separate sections. For example, Time and Death dominate the imagery of the second section, but Death does not appear at all in the first. What dominates the third section, if anything does?

The fact that the imagery alters as the poem progresses should alert you to the fact that this tripartite division of the poem is of considerable significance. Again, it is not the patterns and style set up at the start of the poem which matter so much as the things that change; the reason for isolating rhyme, metre, imagery and all the other techniques is to let you see when a poem is moving on to another target, or changing deliberately, or simply losing its grip. This ability to see beyond the immediate fact staring you in the face is a vital asset for a student of literature: in effect it is the capacity for independent thought, for presenting the examiner with a deduction as well as a statement.

By this stage of the proceedings you should be starting to gain a general idea of the poem's main theme or statement – if, of course, it has one. It is *essential* to realise that this overall grasp of a poem's aims and achievement is not gained the instant you set sight on the poem; it is something that you work towards gradually, and a rash, instant decision that a poem or any other literary extract is trying to achieve a certain aim or effect is prone to disaster – even in an examination where time is short. Let the words work on you before jumping to a conclusion.

A reasonable answer to the question might be along the lines of the specimen answer below, which uses the 'thinking-out-loud' of the plan as a basis and adds to it. You might begin your essay by placing the poem in its context, provided you are fairly certain about this. This is where wide reading shows its advantage. The poem, by Andrew Marvell, is Metaphysical, and could be recognised as such by anyone who was familiar with the two descriptions of Metaphysical poetry given in this Handbook. It is one thing to persuade an examiner you can understand and comment on a poem; it is a decided bonus to suggest to him you are well-read as well.

Answer: The diction and language of the poem suggest a seventeenth-century poet of the Metaphysical school. The subject of the poem is love of a sexual nature between the poet and his mistress; it is phrased in the form of an argument, employs conceits or fanciful imagery, combines reason and passion, and shows considerable wit, all of which suggest the Metaphysical school of writing.

The poem is written in iambic tetrameters for the most part, with occasional departures from this pattern in individual feet. The departures are sometimes for variety ('And the/last Age . . .'), but sometimes appear to be there in order to enhance the sense of the words being used, as in 'hurrying near' and 'ecchoing song'. The regularity of the metre in general gives an ordered, composed tone to the poem, as does the straightforward *aabbcc* rhyme scheme, suggestive of experience recollected in tranquility, rather than experience presented in the first fire of action. The diction is simple yet elevated, without gross use of colloquial language.

The poem is divided into three sections and is written in the form of an argument to the poet's mistress that she should allow him her favours. The first section suggests what might happen if the two lovers had all the time in the world, and to make his point the poet imagines a ludicrously extended period of courtship, including the lines,

An hundred years should go to praise
Thine Eyes, and on thy Forehead Gaze.
Two hundred to adore each Breast;
But thirty thousand to the rest.

After the sexuality implicit in 'Breast' the reader is expecting more specific description of erotic areas; instead, they are simply described as 'the rest', but the time span allotted for their adoration suggests their vast importance.

The second section recognises that humanity is mortal, and that Time is always eating away at a person's life, bringing him nearer to death. There is more dry but rather morbid humour here, in the comment that couples do not embrace in the grave. The third section presents the conclusion. If we had all the time in the world we could take as long as we wished and as was proper to woo each other; we do not have much time; therefore we must act now,

> And tear our Pleasures with rough strife
> Thorough the Iron Gates of life.

There is a sudden injection of violence into the poem in this last section, and urgency and passion that are not present in the same mixture in the preceding two sections. The 'birds of prey' image takes the reader away from the world of languid lovers into a world of harsh reality where pleasure and time are both in short supply. Timelessness dominates the first section, and an awareness of how short man's life is dominates the second section. The third section is dominated by images of violence and action.

Superficially this is a love poem, but the final lines

> Thus, though we cannot make our Sun
> Stand still, yet we will make him run

suggest that sexual love is only the excuse to present a poem which is in effect about mortality, the grip that time holds over man's life, and the shortness of his time on earth. Thus though the poem is written in the first person, the reader learns very little about the author, who remains a representative figure – as does his mistress. The 'I' of the poem can speak for all men because he is not identified with any one particular person. The mood of the poem brushes with the tragic in the final lines, in that defeat is shown as inevitable for mankind, in the sense that all people will die; but this is counteracted by a feeling of exultancy, that even though time will win in the end, there are some things that it can never remove completely, and time, by its inevitability alone, should not be allowed to break man's spirit.

Conclusion: The final version, as given above, has moved a long way from the initial thoughts generated by the poem – which is exactly as it should be. A general essay question often starts from a general statement and moves on to demanding specific proof; a question on a poem works the opposite way round, starting with detail and working up to a general conclusion.

Question 2

Write an appreciation of the poem below:

Strange Meeting

It seemed that out of battle I escaped
Down some profound dull tunnel, long since scooped
Through granites which titanic wars had groined.
Yet also there encumbered sleepers groaned,
Too fast in thought or death to be bestirred.
Then, as I probed them, one sprang up, and stared
With piteous recognition in fixed eyes,
Lifting distressful hands as if to bless.
And by his smile, I knew that sullen hall,
By his dead smile I knew we stood in Hell.
With a thousand pains that vision's face was grained;
Yet no blood reached there from the upper ground,
And no guns thumped, or down the flues made moan.
'Strange friend,' I said, 'here is no cause to mourn.'
'None,' said that other, 'save the undone years,
The hopelessness. Whatever hope is yours,
Was my life also; I went hunting wild
After the wildest beauty in the world,
Which lies not calm in eyes, or braided hair,
But mocks the steady running of the hour,
And if it grieves, grieves richlier than here.
For of my glee might many men have laughed,
And of my weeping something had been left,
Which must die now. I mean the truth untold,
The pity of war, the pity war distilled.
Now men will go content with what we spoiled,
Or, discontent, boil bloody, and be spilled.
They will be swift with swiftness of the tigress.
None will break ranks, though nations trek from progress.
Courage was mine, and I had mystery,
Wisdom was mine, and I had mastery:
To miss the march of this retreating world
Into vain citadels that are not walled.
Then, when much blood had clogged their chariot-wheels,
I would go up and wash them from sweet wells,
Even with truths that lie too deep for taint.
I would have poured my spirit without stint
But not through wounds; not on the cess of war.
Foreheads of men have bled where no wounds were.

I am the enemy you killed, my friend.
I knew you in this dark: for so you frowned
Yesterday through me as you jabbed and killed.
I parried; but my hands were loath and cold.
Let us sleep now . . . .'

Advice: The poem is written in the first person. It uses half-rhyme
('escaped/scooped', 'groined/groaned'), and is clearly based on war.
The opening lines suggest that the author 'escaped' out of battle, and
then suggest that his escape was into Hell; this alone suggests that the
escape is in fact the escape of death, and that the author figure has been
killed in battle. The author figure meets a strange figure who delivers a
long speech that takes up most of the poem. The speaker appears to
believe that he is like the author figure, and that his own death robbed
him of the opportunity to tell the truth about war, '. . . the truth
untold,/The pity of war, the pity war distilled.' The speaker then
suggests he would in some manner have cleansed the world of war.
Finally, he stated 'I am the enemy you killed, my friend', and the poem
closes on a request from the speaker for sleep.

The above gives a 'plot summary' of the poem, of the type that the
student has to make before he can embark on his answer. As an *answer*
the above would be as bad as useless; all it does is talk the reader through
the poem, posing as many questions as it answers. When the first process
of familiarisation with the poem has taken place (in simpler language,
when the student has read it and thought about it for a short while),
basic questions have to be asked. An easy plan could be constructed
using this systematic question-and-answer technique:

Metre? Basically iambic pentameters, with occasional variation, and the
occasional heavy caesura.

Imagery? Not particularly geared to war, though the topic itself is
mentioned, and guns. War imagery not merely modern war imagery
('Chariot wheels', 'vain citadels'). Faces and facial expressions
mentioned several times, and particularly at start and end of poem.
Almost biblical element in imagery?

Diction? As above – biblical in parts. Most of poem cast in monologue
form but diction *not* colloquial – if anything, rather heightened,
formal, elevated.

Rhyme? Strong half-rhyme. Effect? Something not quite right, feeling of
something incomplete? Gives poem very distinctive sound; makes
speech in it rather more artificial, unreal?

Theme? Vision of Hell, life after death? Who is the speaker and who is
the sleeper? Obvious answer: the 'sleeper' is a dead German soldier
killed by poet earlier ('I am the enemy you killed, my friend'). Could
sleeper be poet's conscience, the non-soldier in him, the opposition to

what he is doing? Or could the sleeper be the poet, the other person be the soldier? Idea of *alter ego*; by fighting as a soldier the poet kills himself as a poet? Could the 'sleeper' be Christ, poem a religious allegory?
Thoughts: Is it a war poem at all? (This question might be asked even if you did know that the poem is by Wilfred Owen, probably the best-known of the poets of the First World War).

Two stages of thought have now been gone through – a preliminary reading and summary of the poem (under timed conditions this could be done mentally), and an attempt to obtain basic answers to basic questions. The next stage is to shape the information into a written answer:

Answer: The author figure in the poem escapes 'out of battle'. This, the reference to 'guns thumped', and various other references to warfare suggest that the author figure is a soldier, and that the poem is one of those written about the First World War. However, the author apparently tries to ensure that the warfare in his poem is not identified with any one particular war. It is 'chariot wheels' that the strange speaker in the poems says he will wash clean of blood, not tanks, and the names of any of the participants in the First World War are not mentioned, but simply 'the enemy'. It therefore appears that the poet wishes his poem to have a universal significance, rather than merely being a poem about the First World War.

The author figure goes underground and then meets a strange figure who speaks for the remainder of the poem. The line 'we stood in Hell' suggests a dream vision, or a vision of death. Some of the diction is almost biblical ('vain citadels', 'sweet wells'), again giving an ancient and universal tone to the lines. Half-rhyme is used throughout the poem ('escaped/scooped', 'groined/groaned'), perhaps giving a suggestion of something incomplete, cut short like the lives of the speakers. There is nothing colloquial or relaxed about either the diction or the metre (based on iambic pentameters), and the whole tone of the poem is elevated and monumental, formal and heightened in its impact.

A particular point of interest in the poem is the identity of the two characters within it. They both call each other 'friend'. An obvious interpretation is that the first speaker is a soldier who 'escapes' the horror of battle by means of death, gaining entry to a land full of the war dead who lie like 'encumbered sleepers'. The 'sleeper' who springs up to greet him is an enemy, someone he killed by bayonet or knife the day before:

I knew you in this dark: for so you frowned
Yesterday through me as you jabbed and killed.

There is equality and forgiveness in death. The carnage of war means that all will die sooner or later, and so the exact moment, nature, and agency of one's death is not a cause for grief or vengeance. The killer and the slain will now sleep side by side, proving the idiocy of war, the false divisions it places between people, and that all men are equal in death.

This is an attractive solution to the poem, but it does not fully explain why the 'encumbered sleeper' speaks at length for most of the poem, or account completely for what he says. There is no obvious reason why an ordinary soldier should go '. . . hunting wild/After the wildest beauty in the world', or why

> For of my glee might many men have laughed,
> And of my weeping something had been left.

A possible answer is that the sleeper might be Christ, or a Christ figure. There is the biblical element already mentioned in the diction. The sleeper lifts his hands 'as if to bless'; he seems to have a prophetic desire to do good in the world, and says,

> I would go up and wash them from sweet wells,
> Even with truths that lie too deep for taint.

The sleeper was 'loath' to parry the author-figure's bayonet thrust, as might be expected from someone intended to represent Christ. The killing of the sleeper by the poet could thus be seen as a symbol of the way in which soldiers, by their killing, are forced to abnegate their humanity, their better Christian selves, and their hopes of salvation.

There is a third possible solution to the respective identities of the two characters in the poem. Perhaps the soldier and the sleeper are two sides of the same personality. By becoming a soldier and allowing himself to fight and to kill, the character effectively 'kills' the poetic and artistic side of his own personality. If the sleeper is the poetic aspect of one character and the soldier another, it would explain why the sleeper meets the soldier with 'piteous recognition'. Literary achievement and fulfilment could be what is meant by the sleeper having gone '. . . hunting wild/After the wildest beauty in the world'. The sleeper sees himself as fitted to tell 'the truth untold'; 'courage', 'mystery', 'wisdom', 'mastery' are all features claimed by the sleeper, and all features which could apply to a poet. If the sleeper is the artistic side of the soldier, then it would explain also why the sleeper is this strangely conciliatory enemy who cannot fight the soldier; he would be fighting himself. 'I am the enemy you killed, my friend' can have a psychological as well as a physical meaning. If this is the case then the poem is about a man at war with himself as a result of his having to bear arms against others. In this light, the poet appears to say that poet and soldier are incompatible, that the one kills the other.

It is possible that the poem operates on all three levels of meaning at the same time, and that it is not necessary to pick out one level as the only true statement made by the poem. However, it is the final interpretation, that which sees the poem as a dramatisation of the conflict within the soldier-poet's mind, that has most evidence to support it.

Part 5

The novel

Talking points

A novel is an extended work of prose fiction. Definitions of the novel abound, from the basic to the highly complex, but the student starting a literature course rarely needs to be able to define a novel: he is told if what he is studying is a novel, and then told to get on and understand it.

The novel is a relatively late arrival on the literary scene. Various works that are more or less closely related to the novel do occur before the eighteenth century, but the English novel effectively starts in the eighteenth century with Daniel Defoe (see below). There are some very practical reasons for this flowering of the novel. A novel is neither acted out nor read out to its audience; it is designed to be read on a one-to-one basis. The technology has to exist, therefore, to print large numbers of a novel, to distribute them to the point of sale, and to sell them sufficiently cheaply to allow people to buy them. Secondly, there have to be enough people able and willing to read to make the whole venture economically worthwhile, printing in any age being a very expensive business. Improvements in printing technology, and an increasingly literate population, allowed the novel to be born and to flourish. There had, of course, been large printings of works in prose before the eighteenth century – religious works and sermons, political pamphlets, and so on – but it took some while for the fictional properties of prose, and its value as a medium for entertainment, to be realised. When this had been achieved, the novel was born, and authors rose to the occasion, especially when political unpopularity caused theatres to close and dramatists such as Henry Fielding (see below) had to find alternative outlets for their writing talents.

There are exceptions to every rule, but the basic rule of novels is that they are prose fiction, and tell a story. Telling a story sounds the simplest of tasks; it is one of the most difficult, and the starting point for criticism of a novel is the *narrative viewpoint* adopted by the author, or the way in which he tells the story. One of the most common and simplest narrative viewpoints is that of the first-person narrator. This is employed when the story is told in the 'I' mode, as if by a character in the novel. This is realistic (it is, after all, the way we see events in our own lives, from the 'I' viewpoint); it brings the reader very close to the character of the narrator, and as a result it can make the narrative very vivid and immediate. The more the reader identifies with the narrator, the more whatever happens to the character affects the reader. The first-person narrative technique is realistic also in terms of other characters. In real life we cannot see 'inside the head' of any other person; instead, we have to guess what they are feeling and thinking from external features, such as what they say, what they do, and how they look. The first-person narrator has to do exactly the same thing with the characters in the novel, just as we would do in our own lives.

The first-person narrative is, however, also a technique that restricts the novel to one viewpoint. For the sake of realism that viewpoint can only be at one place at one time. A first-person narrator can only tell the reader about things that would naturally be known to one person. He or she does not have the freedom to go everywhere and see everything. The first-person narrative gives the worm's-eye view. There are times when the bird's-eye view is necessary or desirable as well, and the first-person narrative does not have this range. There is therefore another technique known as that of the *omniscient narrator*. This is when a novel's story is told in the third person, the 'he/she' mode; the narrator is 'omniscient' in that he or she knows everything, can go anywhere at any time, and is not restricted to one viewpoint. The first-person narrative is subjective, personal; the omniscient narrative is apparently objective, detached.

There is considerable confusion over the exact meaning of the term 'omniscient narrator'. It can be a narrator who is both omniscient and invisible – that is, the narrator never appears in the novel, never says anything, and never imposes his own judgement on anything. All the reader has is an apparently factual account of incidents that took place, and details of what people said and did. Or there can be the situation where the above is true for most of the novel, but occasionally the narrator – often assumed to be the novelist, but by no means necessarily so – actually appears to say something and comment directly on the events and experiences that are being written about. Early novels sometimes have a narrator who not only tells the story but also takes time to lecture the reader, share opinions with him, and tell him what he should be thinking, so that the narrator effectively becomes another character in the novel. As a general rule the later the novel the more objective, impersonal, and omniscient the narrative technique is likely to be. Between the two extremes of the first-person narrative and the omniscient narrator a vast range of technique is possible. Two unusual examples of narrative technique are discussed below.

Wuthering Heights

Emily Brontë (1818–48) published *Wuthering Heights* in 1847. It is a remarkable novel. The basic story is of the Earnshaws, a farming family

in the wild moorlands of North Yorkshire, England. On a trip to the city
Father Earnshaw brings back with him a young, wild orphan boy called
Heathcliff. Heathcliff is hated and reviled by the family, falls violently in
love with the daughter of the house, Cathy, and sets out to win Cathy
and ruin the Earnshaw family. The story and the novel are wild, fierce,
and utterly compelling. The actual plot of the novel contains many
events which are seemingly improbable. Emily's solution is to have the
story narrated largely by one Nellie Dean, the practical, down-to-earth,
and reliable servant of the Earnshaw family, who has witnessed most of
the events that take place. She tells this story not to the reader, but to
Lockwood, an effete young city man who is in the area for a holiday and
who rents a house from Heathcliff. The effect of having the events
narrated to us through Nellie and Lockwood is two-fold. Firstly, it aids
the story from the point of view of credibility. If Nellie says something
happened, then we know better than to argue, because she is the type of
person who never exaggerates, never lies, and never believes anything
unless it happens directly in front of her own eyes. The fact that a man
such as Lockwood believes her adds to our own belief as well. Secondly,
it enlarges the narrative potential. The fact that Lockwood arrives on
the scene very near the end of the story arouses suspense, and the reader
soon wishes to find out what gave rise to the extraordinary situation
Lockwood finds at the start of the novel; meanwhile the telling of the
story through the first-person narrative gives it immediacy and
vividness – these are not mere events that we hear about, but things that
actually happened either to or near a real person whom we can hear
speaking. The narrative has the added advantage of being a story told
somewhat after the event, so Nellie has been able to find out certain
things which she might not have known at the actual time things took
place. This is a novel where the restricted range of the first-person
narrative is used to full advantage; it adds to a feeling of claustrophobia,
of being locked in with events, that is a powerful ingredient in the novel's
atmosphere.

Bleak House

Charles Dickens (1812–70) published *Bleak House* in 1853. It is told by
two narrators. There is a first-person narrative by Esther Summerson, a
young girl caught up on the fringe of the great events in the novel, and an
omniscient narrator who gives details of an apparently separate story
which comes closer and closer to Esther's narrative as the novel
proceeds. The two narrators have roughly alternate sections. In one
sense this is an obvious compromise. First-person and omniscient
narration both have advantages, so it seems to make sense to have one of
each in a novel, and thus to gain all the advantages of both techniques

with none of the disadvantages. It is generally a success, although Esther's narrative does reveal one of the weaknesses of the first-person technique. It is essential for the story that Esther is shown to be a good character; but when a person is recounting everything that happens herself, how can she tell the reader about compliments paid to her without sounding insufferably smug and conceited? Dickens solves the problem by making it clear (in the eyes of sympathetic readers) that Esther needs to reassure herself all the time that she is worth something, because she is an orphan who has been deprived of love; but a number of readers believe that Esther is one of the least satisfactory elements in the novel. It is a tribute to Dickens's skill that this is the only problem in his dual narrative technique. It requires vast skill to keep authorial control over two separate narratives that have to retain their own identities without conflicting, and which have to be brought together increasingly as the novel proceeds. The real danger, of course, is that the novel will split into two separate pieces of writing, a weakness from which it could never recover.

Telling the story has more to it than just the type of narrator used by the novelist. Much depends on the type of story the novelist wants – the relationship between plot and character. Early novels tended to feature the PICARESQUE style (see 'Literary Terms' below), whereby the plot was based round a central character. The plot was simply the things that happened to this character, more often than not arranged in a good–bad sequence: first something pleasant would happen, then something unpleasant, and so on. Whilst comparatively easy to write, this type of plot tends to be rambling. At the other extreme is the plot in which a small group of characters meet and mingle throughout the length of the novel, and the incidents take second place to characterisation. If nothing else, this illustrates the intimate link that exists between plot and characterisation in a novel.

Characterisation is another major area in the novel, and a basic area to study for the student coming to terms with a novel. In the early novel characterisation was through external features. The reader was shown what a character did, how he looked, and what he said, and formed his judgements from this information, exactly the same type of information he would receive about characters in real life. It was not until the late Victorian age that novelists began to go inside the heads of their characters, and tell the reader what a character was thinking and feeling at any given moment. Up to this time the reader's knowledge of a character's feelings and thoughts went entirely upon what they said and did, the external symbols and signs only being used by or available to the novelist. When Henry Fielding wrote *Tom Jones* in 1749 he had to express his hero's inner turmoil and agony by showing him quite literally tearing out his hair, an incident that can appear ludicrous. The conventions of the day did not allow Fielding to go inside Tom Jones's head and describe his feelings exactly, as a modern novelist would do. At the other extreme is James Joyce's *A Portrait of the Artist as a Young Man* (1916) in which the character's thoughts are not only described, but done so in the language of the exact age at which he is when the incidents in question take place. From being barred completely from internal psychological narrative, the pendulum had swung to the extent that the novelist was now giving the reader nothing else.

Dialogue is clearly an essential weapon in the novelist's armoury, for purposes of characterisation but also sometimes for the purpose of carrying forward the story. Listen to a group of ordinary people talking. You will hear that they rarely speak in complete sentences; that they interrupt each other continually; that they keep on mouthing non-grammatical phrases such as 'er', 'mmm', 'well!', 'really?', and 'y'know'; that often what they say does not make complete sense. The novelist's job is to show the reader people speaking in an apparently convincing, realistic manner, but at the same time to turn oral language into comprehensible written speech. Immediately the novelist starts to write down speech he is in trouble, because oral and written language are two separate disciplines, and he has to do the latter whilst giving the appearance of the former. Some authors are famous for their skill in writing dialogue; others are infamous. Perhaps the student should be left to make his own mind up about how skilful the novelist he is studying manages to be.

Although any such statement is likely to raise howls of protest from all sorts of people, the novel is usually the easiest of the literary genres for a student to cope with. He is not having to make allowances all the time for something that he should see but can only read, as often happens with drama, and he is not having to decipher close-packed information conveying complex themes by means of complex technical devices, as he sometimes is with poetry. True, a novel can sometimes look daunting simply because of its length, particularly if it is an older novel by an author such as Dickens, but that length can be an advantage if it means that the themes of the novel are spread out and therefore easier to perceive. It is worth bearing in mind that Dickens's novels were published in instalments, usually monthly or fortnightly, and when reading a Dickens novel for the first time it is often a good idea not to try to read the novel in a series of long sittings, but instead to read it instalment by instalment, as its original readership read it. When reading any novel take care not to assume that it can be swallowed in one gulp, as a poem or even a play sometimes can; read it in digestible chunks, or you stand in danger of choking on the whole.

Literary terms

autobiography: a personal account of a person's life; a biography written by the person whose life is described.

biography: an account of someone's life, non-fictional in nature. Modern biographies tend to be scrupulously accurate, at least as regards events. Early biographies were often written to augment or support a particular line of thought, and so the moral of a person's life became more important than the life itself.

flashback: a technique whereby the author interrupts the main narrative to relate events that took place at some time preceding the main narrative.

Gothic novel: the Gothic novel was popular in the late eighteenth and early nineteenth centuries. When early authors used the term 'Gothic' what was often meant was 'medieval', but the term came to be associated with novels that were sensational, supernatural thrillers set in remote castles or monasteries, full of violence and mystery. In many respects these novels were the forerunner of the modern horror film; some of them have indeed been used as the basis for such films. Horace Walpole's *The Castle of Otranto* (1764) is generally acknowledged to be the first Gothic novel; the best (or at least the most thought-provoking) is Mary Shelley's *Frankenstein* (1817).

novella: a work of prose fiction between a short story and a full novel in length.

picaresque: in Spanish the *picaro* was a rogue or villain. The term 'picaresque novel' traditionally refers to a novel with a central figure, the *picaro*, who is low-born, a rogue or knave, and who goes through a sequence of adventures (often unconnected episodes) which are often a vehicle for satire. Details of low life are often realistic and bawdy. *Moll Flanders* by Daniel Defoe (1660–1731) is one example of an English picaresque novel; other novels, such as *Tom Jones* by Henry Fielding (1707–54) appear to be heavily influenced by the style, whilst not being picaresque novels in the strictest sense of the word.

plot: a story or narrative of events.

stream of consciousness: the stream of consciousness technique in novel writing attempts to recreate the actual flow, pattern, and sense of thoughts as they pass through a character's head in real life, or to describe experience as it is actually felt by a person as it is taking place. A character's thoughts, feelings, and impressions are given as they pass through his or her head, and because it is thoughts that are being described logic and grammatical structure are not adhered to, the writing following a pattern of association rather than a pattern of formal speech. James Joyce (1882–1941) and Virginia Woolf (1882–1941) are two of the best-known exponents of the technique in English novel writing.

History and reading list

Group 1: The early novel

There were a number of works which had more than a passing hint of the novel in them before the eighteenth century. After Daniel Defoe (1660–1731) there was no doubt that the English novel had been born. Defoe was as fascinating a character as he is a novelist. In common with many other early novelists he turned to novel writing almost by accident, in the course of an extraordinarily varied and productive life. He was at various times a merchant, a journalist, a pamphleteer, and a spy; he wrote something approaching five hundred separate works (only a fraction of these being novels), was rendered bankrupt after being pilloried and imprisoned, and surrounded himself with an air of mystery that not even modern biographers have managed to penetrate. His best-known works are *Robinson Crusoe* (1719), and *Moll Flanders* (1722). *Robinson Crusoe* is based on the true story of Alexander Selkirk, a sailor marooned on a desert island for a number of years. *Moll Flanders* tells the story of a woman who is a thief, a criminal, and virtually a prostitute, and who finally makes her fortune in the New World. Defoe narrates the most remarkable incidents in the most matter-of-fact style, and this factual, pseudo-documentary style is a major feature of his writing. His books are rambling and relatively disorganised, but Defoe's humanity, sense of humour, and the sheer liveliness of his mind compensate for this. Defoe was an optimist; Moll Flanders is allowed to die (we presume) in her own respectable bed, and Robinson Crusoe survives his experience very well, whilst the original Alexander Selkirk came out of it all much less well.

Samuel Richardson (1689–1761) is another famous figure in the early history of the English novel. An apprentice printer, he married his employer's daughter and eventually came to own the firm. Richardson pioneered a new form of writing, almost by accident. He was commissioned to publish and write a book of specimen letters for literate but badly-educated people who did not know the correct forms to use when writing letters. From this developed Richardson's first novel, *Pamela* (1740), which is told in the form of letters from Pamela, a young maidservant whose mistress has just died at the opening of the story. Pamela finds herself the object of an all-out attempt at seduction by her ex-mistress's son. She resists tenaciously and as a result marries the son. The novel has aroused fierce criticism, largely because of its morality. The lust of Pamela's seducer is seen as a sin before marriage, but presumably the marriage service does not alter the passion; it is still lust, and a sin, but in some strange way is now respectable. Similarly, Pamela can appear very calculating; an 'A' level student once wrote that 'the moral of *Pamela* is that if you refuse to have intercourse with a man for long enough you will drive him sufficiently mad for him to marry you.' Pamela can seem very self-satisfied, very calculating, and rather immoral in her impeccable morality. On the other hand, Richardson's use of the letter technique allowed a much closer and more complex characterisation than was possible by the use of more conventional techniques such as that used by Defoe, and in this sense Richardson is nearer to twentieth-century novelists than the majority of his eighteenth-century counterparts, for most of whom plot was marginally more significant than characterisation. Richardson's dialogue is also good, but it is his characterisation that has given rise to him being hailed as the founder of the modern novel. *Clarissa* (1747) is a gloomier and more pessimistic novel; some would argue it is superior to *Pamela*.

No-one would argue with the claim that Henry Fielding (1707–54) is one of the commanding figures of the eighteenth-century novel. As did Defoe, he came to novel writing almost by accident, when political action closed the theatres and stopped him from writing plays. Fielding was a dramatist, a journalist, a lawyer, and a minor magistrate, as well as a novelist, and is in many respects at the opposite extreme to Richardson. Indeed, Fielding's early prose efforts, and in particular his novel *Joseph Andrews* (1742), were directed at satirising Richardson, whose morality he found unacceptable. *Joseph Andrews* starts off as a direct parody of Richardson, with Joseph (Pamela's brother) fleeing from attempted seduction by his employer, Lady Booby. However, half-way through Fielding forgets he is writing a satire, and starts to write a novel in its own right, with the hero becoming the comic but hugely appealing Parson Adams. In 1749 Fielding published what is certainly his greatest work, and one of the greatest of all English novels, *Tom Jones*. The plot has its roots in the PICARESQUE style (see 'Literary Terms' above), but is more organised than is usually the case with picaresque works, and follows a highly logical, symmetrical pattern. The hero, Tom Jones, reveals Fielding's morality with rich simplicity. A man of the world, Fielding was much more concerned with the spirit rather than the letter, of the law. His hero makes mistakes, and he is punished for them, but because his heart is in the right place, and because he never willingly or knowingly sets out to hurt anyone, he is forgiven and rewarded with all the novelist can muster. Fielding is concerned with people's feelings, and not a profit-and-loss account of what they have done and what they have not done. Fielding's morality is complex, more so than can adequately be suggested in such short notes as these. He is not a writer who condones sin; he can understand it and forgive it. *Tom Jones* also contains the utterly memorable Squire Western, one of the most powerfully comic characters of the eighteenth-century novel as a whole. Fielding described *Tom Jones* as a 'comic epic in prose', a statement which reveals both its nature, and Fielding's nervousness about the novel form – his claim that it is an epic is partly an attempt to make it respectable and in line with classical models. Like Defoe, Fielding is a compassionate, liberal writer whose liveliness of mind matches his humanity.

One other novelist and one other novel demand attention. The novelist is Tobias Smollett (1721–71), author of *Roderick Random* (1748), *Peregrine Pickle* (1751), and *Humphry Clinker* (1771), among others. Smollett is a violent, boisterous writer, crude by comparison with Fielding both in terms of plot and characterisation, but his novels are worth reading for their energy, and use of the picaresque technique.

The novel is *Tristram Shandy* (1767) by Laurence Sterne (1713–68). Superficially the novel is an exercise in anarchy, with a plot that never seems to get near being started until a third of the way through, bizarre characterisation, a narrator as confused as his readers, and all sorts of tricks to perplex (and delight) the reader – wriggly lines showing the direction of the plot, blank pages, black pages. Beneath this anarchic surface the novel has a deep human sympathy, a rich comic texture, and an impishness and joy in flouting convention that have ensured its survival over the years.

Reading list
TEXTS:
Fielding, *Tom Jones.*
Defoe, *Moll Flanders.*

CRITICISM:
I. Watt, *The Rise of the Novel.*

Group 2: Scott, Austen and the Brontës

This group of writers flourished in the first half of the nineteenth century, but apart from this there is very little to link them, and their grouping together is an administrative convenience rather than a reflection of any literary similarity. Sir Walter Scott (1771–1832) was an extremely successful author in his own day, but has fallen out of fashion in modern times. His novels are sometimes set by examination boards, and he was a pioneer as regards the historical novel, or novel that deals with an age set back in time from the author's own time. Scott started life as a lawyer, progressed to being a poet, and then when his poetry was overshadowed by that of Byron, turned to novel-writing. Among his better-known works are the so-called 'Waverley' novels, starting with *Waverley* (1814), *Ivanhoe* (1819), *Rob Roy* (1818), *Redgauntlet* (1824), *The Heart of Midlothian* (1818), *Old Mortality* (1816), and *Guy Mannering* (1815). Scott is best when writing of Scotland, and using the

Scottish folk-tales and stories he was familiar with from his youth. His vast output of novels is partly explained by the fact that a publishing company with which he was involved went bankrupt, and Scott vowed to pay off all creditors by his exertions. He lived in some splendour on the Abbotsford estate, the realisation of a personal dream. Scott's novels can be 'thin' for modern critical taste – thematically quite lightweight, and relying heavily on plot to carry them through – but they have considerable charm; and perhaps the criticism of 'thinness' is more of a comment on the changing nature of taste and society than Scott has been given credit for. His novels are certainly well worth reading.

No-one would question the value of reading the novels of Jane Austen (1775–1817). She published only six novels: *Sense and Sensibility* (1811), *Pride and Prejudice* (1813), *Mansfield Park* (1814), *Emma* (1816), and *Northanger Abbey* and *Persuasion* (1818). Jane Austen led a secluded life with her family, never marrying. Her novels have as their subject country landed gentry, with a social range that touches the aristocracy (or at least the aristocracy of the countryside) at its topmost range, and never falls significantly below upper middle class. It is a small sector of society, and her subject matter – more often than not a young girl who is about to marry, or at least ready for it – makes her novels even more restricted. World events do not impinge on Jane Austen's world, and an invitation to a ball is more important than the doings of Bonaparte in Europe. Jane Austen was aware herself of the narrow range of her novels, and took the line that it was better for her to do what she did well rather than try her hand at areas in which she might have less success. Her novels do indeed succeed because of their excellence, and because her characters are universally human, their particular social class being a thin veneer over features that are of universal significance. Manners matter greatly in Jane Austen's code of morality: behaviour must be and has to be controlled, even if feelings cannot be so regulated. The character who wears his or her heart on a sleeve, the person who cannot exercise restraint, these are the people condemned in her novels. Jane Austen strives for a civilised standard of behaviour. If this means control of feeling, it also means the application of common sense: Jane Austen does not argue with people who marry for love – as long as there is at least some money there as well. She is neither heartless, nor callous, nor mercenary; prudence and caution are perhaps more suitable words. Her novels have a precise structure, an extremely skilful and deft use of irony, and recreate a certain pattern of life extremely vividly. She may not question as much as many of her contemporaries, but she reveals and comments with great sharpness, wit, and accuracy.

Jane Austen and the Brontë sisters could not be further apart. The Brontë family were brought up in relative isolation in the village of Haworth in North Yorkshire, where their eccentric father was the local clergyman. Their mother died when they were young, and the family were brought up by their aunt, an unwilling traveller from the south of England who rarely left her room. With the moors on the one hand and their father's library on the other, the young children began to invent and write about their own fantasy worlds. Maria and Elizabeth Brontë died in their infancy in 1824. Branwell Brontë (1817–48), the only male child, died of tuberculosis and alcoholism in his early thirties, and Emily (1818–48) died a short while afterwards. Anne (1820–49) died in the following year, and Charlotte (1816–55) was to die only a year after her marriage. This tragic story of early death and family suffering and the magnificent setting of Haworth have created something of a personality cult around the Brontë family, but this also springs from the novels that they wrote, and in particular two novels – *Wuthering Heights* (1847) by Emily, and *Jane Eyre* (1847) by Charlotte. *Wuthering Heights* has already been discussed in terms of its plot and narrative structure (see pp. 111–12). The novel is almost tragic in its scope, dealing in good and evil rather than good and bad, and with an elemental and primitive force in it that can hardly be matched in any other novel; at times it seems to operate on its own internal morality that rises above mundane, everyday concerns. Psychologists have commented that the book's power is based on adolescent sexuality, moulded by repression and innocence; critics have commented on the links with Shakespeare's *King Lear* and the GOTHIC NOVEL (see 'Literary Terms' above); ordinary people have commented consistently over the years with their purses by buying the novel in tens of thousands. It has lost little of its power to attract over the years, and Heathcliff, its central character, is now a household word, ranking in this respect at least alongside characters such as Hamlet. *Jane Eyre* has also been consistently popular, but perhaps to a lesser degree than *Wuthering Heights*. *Jane Eyre* is autobiographical to the extent that it relies on Charlotte's experiences as a governess and the humiliation she felt in this post, but it is also wish or dream fulfilment on a grand scale. It is at once the Cinderella or rags-to-riches story, a moral tract, and novel of passion and mystery. Its dialogue is very weak, even clumsy, and the plot relies on at least one highly improbable incident; but sheer imaginative drive and power rescue the novel from melodrama, and make it compelling reading. Charlotte also wrote *Shirley* (1849), *Villette* (1853), and *The Professor* (1857), but none of these has had the popular success of *Jane Eyre*.

This period of literature lacked nothing in variety. At one extreme is Jane Austen, standing for elegance, control, and civilisation; at the other stands Emily Brontë, in full flight for passion, emotion, and a wild Romanticism. The student who wishes to have illustrated the difference between the Classical and the Romantic outlook need only read *Emma* and follow it by *Wuthering Heights*.

Group 3: Dickens, Thackeray, Eliot and Trollope

The middle third of the nineteenth century saw the peak of the novel's popularity, and the major figure in this popularity was Charles Dickens (1812–70). Dickens is a difficult author to write about in a short space of time. Firstly, he is so much the accepted genius of the English novel that he is, like Shakespeare, an institution, and literary institutions can breed a very natural resentment on the part of students – a resentment that is fuelled by the remaining difficulties. Secondly, in common with a number of other great writers, he suffers from the fact that his worst works, such as *A Tale of Two Cities* (1859), are often taught in schools. Thirdly, he is an adult writer, and many a student has been put off Dickens by being introduced to him at too young an age.

Dickens's life is straightforward. The son of a pleasant but wholly ineffectual clerk who was imprisoned for debt, Dickens was sent out as a child to work in a factory, an experience which totally humiliated and degraded him and left him with a permanent mental scar, the traces of which can be seen in the frequency with which the figures of lost, neglected, or maltreated children appear in his novels. With a little education and a great deal of hard work Dickens became a Parliamentary reporter, then a form of journalist, and eventually a published novelist. The majority of his novels were published in serial form, in monthly or fortnightly instalments, and at times he had three novels in progress as well as numerous other activities. His popularity varied from the immense to the merely vast, and though his sales figures dipped with certain novels, this never persisted long enough to form a pattern. His popularity also survived his separation from his wife relatively late in his life. Dickens was never an intellectual (one critic has described the theme of every Dickens novel as being that 'people should be nicer to one another'), and was always in close touch with his readers, who spanned the whole of society. He was an actor of some genius, and was heavily involved in amateur theatricals for much of his life, pursuing this activity with almost frantic energy. Later he began to give extremely successful public readings from his works, and the strain of these was to play no small part in his relatively early death. It is possible that both his acting and his readings sprang from a need to gain the support and encouragement of his audience at first-hand, to hear his success in the form of actual live applause.

With any such figure a selection from his novels is bound to leave glaring gaps, but his first major successful novel, *Pickwick Papers* (1837) demands attention. Loosely organised, comic, but with a developing seriousness in its later stages, the novel, with the character, was a publishing phenomenon, launching Dickens into the Victorian equivalent of stardom. *Oliver Twist* (1838) followed, with its story of an orphan boy subjected to the horrors of criminal life in London. Of his middle period *Dombey & Son* (1848) and *David Copperfield* (1850) are possibly the most noteworthy, the former for its realism and control, the latter for its strong autobiographical element. Of the final period, *Bleak House* (1853) is a savage attack on the law and English society, whilst *Great Expectations* (1861) is arguably his most successful work, featuring the growth into maturity of Philip ('Pip') Pirrip by means of snobbery, infatuation, and finally self-knowledge. The blend of a strong narrative line, hard realism blurring into symbolic fantasy, and a conclusion poised between optimism and pessimism all contribute to the novel's success. *Our Mutual Friend* (1865) was Dickens's last complete novel. It illustrates the effects of money on society and individuals within society and is, in effect, a satire on a society which worships money. Powerful as it is, it is probably not the book for a student who wishes to gain a preliminary knowledge of Dickens.

Modern criticism has favoured the later novels by Dickens; but his own age never quite relinquished a tendency to lament the passing of the author of *Pickwick Papers*, and complain at the growing sombre element in his work. In any event, Dickens's reputation has survived changes in fashion, and his work has been a mainstay of film and television producers. Characters such as Fagin from *Oliver Twist* and Mr Micawber from *David Copperfield* (a portrait based on Dickens's own father) have passed into folk lore and become household names, used by people who have never read a Dickens novel in their lives. The same cannot be said of Dickens's main contemporary rival, William Makepeace Thackeray (1811–63). Thackeray came within a whisker of illustrating *Pickwick Papers* for Dickens, and, being a talented illustrator, was never as committed to the novel as was Dickens. Though a prolific writer he is known nowadays mainly for his novel *Vanity Fair* (1848), a frank, satirical, and sometimes world-weary portrait of the top level of society as Thackeray saw it. It contains the superb, sharply drawn character Becky Sharp, a girl with nothing but her good looks, intelligence, and utter ruthlessness to see her through life. Her total immorality eventually results in her social downfall, though only after prodigious success: she is a telling comment on the double standards of society. Thackeray manages to suggest that he is totally bored with the good characters in his novel and at the same time generates huge sympathy and affection for them. His stance in *Vanity Fair* is to pretend to be amused by the idiocy of society; he never quite succeeds in hiding the fact that he is hurt as well.

Another famous name from the period is that of George Eliot (1819–80), in real life Mary Ann Evans. Her best-known novels are *Adam Bede* (1859), *The Mill on the Floss* (1860), *Silas Marner* (1861), *Middlemarch* (1872), and *Daniel Deronda* (1876). *Middlemarch* is the one undoubted masterpiece. George Eliot has great powers of psychological subtlety, a firm pattern of intellectual enquiry, but also a tendency to send a novel in different directions at the same time, become a little too serious, symbolic, and intellectual, and in general give critics anxious to 'place' her something of a headache. Her novels deserve to be listed among the famous because of their characterisation, and in this area alone she was a significant influence on the development of the novel.

Finally, room has to be found for Anthony Trollope (1815–82), who has been described as a 'male Jane Austen'. His novels of clerical life, the best-known of which is probably *Barchester Towers* (1857) have an ease and wit that few other novelists can reach. He is underestimated by modern criticism, but in common with Jane Austen he did a small thing very well.

Reading list
TEXTS:
Dickens, *Oliver Twist*
    Great Expectations
Thackeray, *Vanity Fair*
George Eliot, *Middlemarch*

Group 4: Hardy, James and Conrad

It is often the case that after a long period in which one or more authors have dominated a particular mode or *genre* there is a period of decline. This is certainly not true of the novel in the period after the domination of Dickens. Thomas Hardy (1840–1928) was the son of a mason; he qualified as an architect, but then turned to writing. His novels are based firmly in his rural county of Dorset, which he disguises in the novels as 'Wessex'. His reputation is based on five novels: *Far From the Madding Crowd* (1874); *The Mayor of Casterbridge* (1886); *Tess of the D'Urbervilles* (1891), and *Jude the Obscure* (1896) are the most notable, with either *The Return of the Native* (1878) or *The Woodlanders* (1887) making the fifth, depending on which critic does the ranking. Hardy's vision is essentially pessimistic. He sees old, time-honoured ways of rural life being demolished by new, industrial ways, and shows how the rural population are sacrificed to progress. There is frequently a malignant Fate or Destiny in his novels that blocks progress for any of his character, swallows ambition, and blinds achievement. The concept is perhaps developed more intellectually in his poetry, where some attempt is made to define the 'Immanent Will' that rules human destiny; it is made clear in the novels by virtue of their pessimism, at its strongest in *Tess of the D'Urbervilles* and *Jude the Obscure*. In the latter novel in particular the pessimism is so strong as to become almost ludicrous at times, and Hardy does have a tendency to let the urgency of what he wants to say obscure the best way of saying it. However, his grip of country life and people, his flair for anecdote and characterisation, and his all-pervading human sympathy are remarkable.

Hardy and Thackeray had in common a resentment against and impatience with the moral strictures of the time which did not allow full and frank discussion of certain areas such as sexuality and sinfulness. For serial publication Hardy had to alter his novels radically to fit in with what it was felt the public would accept; in one instance he even had to delete an incident where a young man carries a girl across a patch of wet ground, and the seduction of Tess in *Tess of the D'Urbervilles* becomes so vague that the reader is unsure as to whether the man has had intercourse with her, or whether she has just fallen asleep. Pressures such as this, and a lifelong affection for poetry, made Hardy change from prose to poetry in his later years.

Hardy's novels are renowned for their proximity to tragedy, and their ability to describe the countryside and its people. Joseph Conrad (1857–1924) was a markedly different figure. Born of a Polish father, he did not learn English until he was twenty years old. He spent a number of years at sea in various merchant navies, and his novels show his knowledge of the sea as a lasting influence. He was, however, dogged by ill health for much of his life. His most famous novels are *The Nigger of the Narcissus* (1898), *Lord Jim* (1900), *Heart of Darkness* (1902) (a short novel), *Nostromo* (1904), *The Secret Agent* (1907), *Under Western Eyes* (1911), and perhaps *Victory* (1915). His early work was marred by his having to come to terms with English; his later years showed a decided falling-off in the standard of his writing. Many of Conrad's novels are based on the classic adventure story but they rarely end at that. He is a master of complex narrative techniques, and such devices as time-shifting and changing viewpoints. He tends to show characters in extreme situations, testing themselves and being tested, not always with success. Conrad is both a Romantic and a modern writer: his search for truth and certainty inside a man, his belief that in the final count it is our own reserves and resources that we lean on, and his fondness for mystery and vague uncertainty are all Romantic. The elements of uncertainty, sense of corruption, and loss of direction and purpose are all very modern. He believes in faithfulness or fidelity as a prime human virtue, and darkness is a potent symbol in his novels. At his worst Conrad presents a vague and rather insubstantial Romanticism; at his best he presents a powerful, mystifying, and symbolic vision of modern man.

A completely different writer is Henry James (1843–1916), an American who became a British citizen shortly before his death. The theme of James's earlier group of novels is that of the innocent American coming into contact with the richer, but also more corrupting culture of Europe. Of his earlier novels, the best-known are probably *Roderick Hudson* (1875), *Washington Square* (1880), and *Portrait of a Lady* (1881), all 'international' novels in the sense that they span two cultures. In later novels – *The Ambassadors* (1903) and *The Golden Bowl* (1904) for example – his technique becomes even more refined and he seems to be moving towards the STREAM OF CONSCIOUSNESS technique (see 'Literary Terms' above). Some critics and readers have felt that James is too refined, too precise, too concerned with style, and that his novels lack the texture of reality; others welcome his advances in technique, and the fine, delicate shading he sought to bring into characterisation. It is sometimes said that his later novels are easier to read if the readers know that they were dictated to a secretary, rather than written down; and certainly they have a very different effect if they are heard, rather than read.

Reading list
TEXTS:
Hardy, *Tess of the D'Urbervilles* or *Far From the Madding Crowd*.
Conrad, *Heart of Darkness*.
James, *Portrait of a Lady*.

Group 6: The modern novel

The term 'modern' has a variety of connotations, and in literary criticism it can mean different things to different people. For the sake of convenience, 'modern' is used here to describe the work of an author whose main writing career fell in the twentieth century. Even then, this only applies in part to an author like H. G. Wells (1866–1946); but it would be strange to claim that the man considered by many to be the founder of the English Science Fiction novel was other than 'modern'.

Wells is something of an enigma. He was capable of turning out two or three books a year, and prolific writers have tended to fare less well in the battle with the critics than writers who have carefully rationed their output. He was a popular writer, perhaps more dictated to by his audience than any writer since Charles Dickens, and a populariser of complex ideas. His reputation rests on two separate strands in his work, the first being his early 'science-fiction' novels (although it should be noted that the term, used now to describe almost any novel set in the future, was not invented until after Wells's death). Wells had an insatiable curiosity and a perceptive although shallow interest in science. His early novels tended to see a possibility in one or more contemporary lines of scientific research, and then use it as the basis for a mildly sensational novel. *The Time Machine* (1895) dealt with time travel, *The Invisible Man* (1897) with invisibility, and *The War of the Worlds* (1898) with an invasion of Earth from Mars. Wells also predicted war in the air and tanks before their actual appearance. The science-fiction novels are rather better than a considerable amount of modern criticism would have the reader believe. *The War of the Worlds* is largely well-written sensationalism, although it was prophetic in more ways than one, anticipating the modern fascination with disasters of a world-wide nature. However, *The Time Machine* says a considerable amount about the future of humanity, and is a deeply thought-provoking novel, as well as a very good story. *The Invisible Man* has a compelling and chilling character sketch at its heart, moves very skilfully from broad comedy to horror, and says a considerable amount about human fear of the outsider, and mob instincts. Wells's other group of novels, typified by *Kipps* (1906), *Tono Bungay* (1909), and *The History of Mr Polly* (1910) are very different indeed. Comic, concerned with human weakness and society rather than great events and science, they are moving, richly-textured, and gently satiric without ever being malicious, and have never lost a wide readership despite relative unfashionableness.

The step from H. G. Wells to D. H. Lawrence (1885–1930) is vast indeed. Late-Victorian reticence is still firmly in control in Wells's novels (even if the same was not true of his private life); it is beaten to death in Lawrence's work. The son of a miner in Nottinghamshire and a mother with intellectual ambitions for her son, Lawrence has become identified with the fight against censorship and for freedom of expression, particularly as his novel *Lady Chatterley's Lover* (1928), with its explicit descriptions of sexual activity and its use of words hitherto thought to be obscene, was used as a test-case in England in the 1960s. Realism, sexuality, freedom of and for the passionate side of human nature all feature largely in Lawrence's work, together with a feeling that modern, civilised life is somehow corrupting man and taking him further and further away from the root sources of his being. His best novels – *Sons and Lovers* (1913), *The Rainbow* (1915), and *Women in Love* (1921) – blend industrial and rural settings magnificently, and breathe out the fire and passion that Lawrence was trying to put back into life. They also hint at his own acute suffering, and, perhaps, the single-mindedness that at one and the same time made him memorable but also just a little limited.

E. M. Forster (1879–1970) was as much of the upper middle class as Lawrence was of the working class, and his life spanned a greater degree of change than that of almost any modern writer except H. G. Wells. Forster was the author of, among other novels, *Where Angels Fear to Tread* (1905), *A Room With a View* (1908), *Howard's End* (1911), and *A Passage to India* (1924). At once anti-Christian, intellectual, detached, ironic, nostalgic, satiric, and comic, it took time for Forster's talent to be recognised, but when it was he was seen as one of the greatest twentieth-century novelists. His stance as an outsider, and as someone who felt strongly the inflexibility of the English, may be explained by his homosexuality, and by his membership of the 'Bloomsbury Group' (see below). Forster also wrote what has become required reading for almost every student of the novel, *Aspects of the Novel* (1927), a highly personal but very worthwhile critical comment on technique and content in the novel.

Virginia Woolf (1882–1941) was also a member of the Bloomsbury Group, a rather grand name given later by critics to a collection of individuals who met in houses in and around the London district of Bloomsbury to exchange ideas, and a haven for intellectuals who otherwise found little support in English society between 1918 and 1939. Virginia Woolf's suicide by drowning in 1941, her extremely 'modern' ideas, and the strange isolation of her life have made her something of an enigma, and a figure of considerable attraction for modern writers. Most students know her through *Mrs Dalloway* (1925), *To the Lighthouse* (1927), and possibly *The Waves* (1931), although the latter novel is usually only studied at a very advanced level. She is concerned with people's inner experience, the intricate working of their minds, and as such adopts a technique close to the STREAM OF CONSCIOUSNESS approach (see 'Literary Terms' above). *Mrs Dalloway* is one day in the life of Mrs Dalloway, although the 'flashback' technique (going back in time) is used to give the reader a fuller picture of the character in question. *To the Lighthouse* is similarly concerned with character and personality, but also with themes of time and change. *The Waves* is remarkable for its style, the most experimental and unconventional of any of her novels.

Virginia Woolf seems fascinated by minute detail, and the shaping forces of character, and as such there are clear links with Henry James (see above), and James Joyce (1882–1941). Joyce, an Irishman who left Ireland to live on the Continent in 1904, was to write one of the most influential novels of the twentieth century: *Ulysses* (1922). He then went on to write work that was virtually unreadable. Joyce's first book was a collection of short stories, *Dubliners*, published in 1914 after considerable troubles over censorship. *A Portrait of the Artist as a Young Man* followed in 1916. This novel is partially autobiographical, telling the story of Stephen Dedalus up to the time of his rejection of the Roman Catholic church and faith. Although not entirely related in the stream of consciousness technique, it is a narrative told from the viewpoint of the one character, and the style used changes as does the imagined age of the narrator. *Ulysses* is generally recognised as Joyce's master work, a stream of consciousness novel divided between a dispirited Stephen Dedalus and his antithesis, a character called Leopold Bloom. Joyce tries to recreate the sound, feel, and pattern of these people's thoughts as they go through their minds on one particular day. The result is in fact a compilation of many styles, and a richly comic novel which can also be extremely moving. Joyce spent the next seventeen years of his life writing *Finnegan's Wake* (1939). It could be argued that this novel's private language and its endless word play show it to have an almost endless number of levels on which it is operating, or that it is simply unreadable. Most students (though not all) find the latter to be the case; but far be it from this Handbook to put any would-be reader off a modern novel.

George Orwell (1903–50) is a novelist blessed or cursed (depending on the reader's viewpoint) by the fact that two of his novels appear as standard items on a large number of examination boards' lists: *Animal Farm* (1945) and *Nineteen Eighty-Four* (1949). *Animal Farm* is an allegorical satire which uses animals and a farm setting to illustrate the corruption and failure of Stalin's rule in Russia – although the novel can also act as a comment on any totalitarian rule. *Nineteen Eighty-Four* is a chilling vision of the future, and a savage comment and prophecy about the inevitable result of totalitarian government. It shows a society in a permanent state of war where government, through fear and the lust for power, has been refined with the aid of technology to a point where the system seems invincible.

Aldous Huxley (1894–1963) is known to students through one book: *Brave New World* (1932). Another vision of the future, this is less chilling at first sight than *Nineteen Eighty-Four*, but eventually equally horrific, showing a society where the pursuit of a mock happiness has robbed humanity of all drive, individuality, and character.

Evelyn Waugh (1906–66) is the greatest satirical novelist of this century. A strange and complex figure, Waugh did more than any other writer to sum up the atmosphere and tone of a certain section of society in Britain between 1925 and 1939. He was 'wild and dissolute' when young, but became a committed Roman Catholic; he poured scorn on society before the Second World War (1939–45), but fought bravely in it; he wrote with occasional sharp cruelty, but could also write with great compassion. His first novel, *Decline and Fall* (1928) is possibly still his best-remembered. It tells of the decline, fall, and eventual resurrection of Paul Pennyfeather, a poor innocent caught up in the anarchy of upper-class life in England between the wars. The novel is biting, sharp, and extremely funny, but also a criticism of society, as is *Vile Bodies* (1930). *Brideshead Revisited* (1945) shows Waugh's movement towards

Catholicism and his growing distrust of modern life. *The Loved One* (1948) deals with the American industry of funeral parlours for humans and animals, and is one of his blackest and most cynical books. *Sword of Honour* (1965), based on a trilogy of novels about the Second World War, is rather more good-natured than his earlier work.

When dealing with authors who are still living the student would be best advised to read their work and make his own mind up on their respective worth, without being influenced by the opinions of critics or the selections of the examiners. Any list of contemporary authors is to a certain extent a personal choice, but included in the list below are some authors whose work has already been selected as set books for examination syllabuses.

Kingsley Amis (*b.*1922) is best known for *Lucky Jim* (1954), perhaps a novel to be linked with the appearance of ANGRY YOUNG MEN (see p. 38) in drama, or perhaps just a comic masterpiece. Lawrence Durrell (*b.*1912) is a complex author, best known for his *Alexandria Quartet* (*Justine* published in 1957, *Balthazar* in 1958, *Mountolive* in 1958, and *Clea* in 1960), works which have been linked with the *Music of Time* series by Anthony Powell (*b.*1905), and novels by C. P. Snow (1905–80), notably the *Strangers and Brothers* series which began in 1935. William Golding (*b.*1911) is justifiably famous for *Lord of the Flies* (1954), a novel about a group of children stranded on a desert island through force of war, who reveal a number of facets of human nature by their behaviour.

Graham Greene (*b.*1904) is perhaps the most respected of all modern novelists. His conversion to Roman Catholicism has been a significant factor in his novel writing. He has an abiding interest in criminals and criminality, in betrayal, and in films: a number of his novels seem to use techniques suitable for the cinema, particularly with their strong visual and narrative elements. Among his best-known works are *Stamboul Train* (1932), *A Gun for Sale* (1936), *The Third Man* (1950), *Our Man in Havana* (1958), *Brighton Rock* (1938), *The Power and the Glory* (1940), and *A Burnt Out Case* (1961). Greene's use of espionage stories and his capacity for making seediness and decay both compelling and frightening have been adopted by several more recent authors. His novels are adventure stories which frequently reveal themselves as moral fables, but fables firmly based in and on real life.

Barry Hines (*b.*1939) is a regional writer, and one with a strong political commitment, and exists somewhere between George Orwell and D. H. Lawrence, but with a reticence about internal psychological narrative and a broad humour that also reminds the reader of certain Victorian novelists. He is best known for *Kes* (1968), and *The Gamekeeper* (1975).

Laurie Lee (*b.*1914) wrote his autobiography *Cider with Rosie* (1959) and has never been off an examination syllabus since; the fact that the novel is still widely-read and admired, even by students who have been examined on it, is the best possible testimony to the worth of the book.

Alan Sillitoe (*b*.1928) invites comparison with Barry Hines as a regional, working-class novelist; he is best-known for *Saturday Night and Sunday Morning* (1958) and *The Loneliness of the Long Distance Runner* (1959).

Reading list
TEXTS:
Wells, *The History of Mr Polly*.
Lawrence, *The Rainbow*.
Forster, *Howard's End*.
Joyce, *Ulysses* or *A Portrait of the Artist as a Young Man*.
Orwell, *Animal Farm*.
Huxley, *Brave New World*.
Waugh, *Decline and Fall*.
Golding, *Lord of the Flies*.
Hines, *Kes*.
Greene, *Brighton Rock*.

Practical criticism and appreciation

In this section passages from three novels, each very different from the others, will be discussed as if the student is being asked to comment on them unseen. The first passage is from *A Portrait of the Artist as a Young Man* by James Joyce:

> Once upon a time and a very good time it was there was a moocow coming down along the road and this moocow that was coming down along the road met a nicens little boy named baby tuckoo ....
>
> His father told him that story: his father looked at him through a glass: he had a hairy face.
>
> He was baby tuckoo. The moocow came down the road where Betty Byrne lived: she sold lemon platt.
>
> *O, the wild rose blossoms*
> *On the little green place.*
>
> He sang that song. That was his song.
>
> *O, the green wothe botheth.*
>
> When you wet the bed first it is warm then it gets cold. His mother put on the oilsheet. That had the queer smell.
>
> His mother had a nicer smell than his father. She played on the piano the sailor's hornpipe for him to dance. He danced:

Tralala lala,
Tralala tralaladdy
Tralala lala,
Tralala lala.

Uncle Charles and Dante clapped. They were older than his father and mother but uncle Charles was older than Dante.

Dante had two brushes in her press. The brush with the maroon velvet back was for Michael Davitt and the brush with the green velvet back was for Parnell. Dante gave him a cachou every time he brought her a piece of tissue paper.

The Vances lived in number seven. They had a different father and mother. They were Eileen's father and mother. When they were grown up he was going to marry Eileen. He hid under the table. His mother said:

– O, Stephen will apologize.
Dante said:
– O, if not, the eagles will come and pull out his eyes. –

Pull out his eyes,
Apologize,
Apologize,
Pull out his eyes.

Apologize,
Pull out his eyes,
Pull out his eyes,
Apologize.

The first reaction to a passage such as this is, quite possibly, going to be sheer horror. If the student recognises that it is written to suggest the workings of a child's mind then all is well; if this fact is not realised, then it is going to be very difficult indeed for the student to gain any marks, however long the answer. As to how the fact is to be recognised, there is no simple answer. It is one of those things which look very simple when explained, but which in the pressure of an examination can be completely overlooked.

The first task in answering a question of this nature is to state the obvious, that the passage seems to be designed to imitate or suggest the thoughts of a child, possibly a five- or six-year-old. The next task is to state the techniques and devices which the author uses to create this effect. They can be listed as follows:

'Once upon a time' is a phrase associated with stories for young children.
'moocow' is a child's name for a cow.
'nicens' is baby talk.

'baby tuckoo' suggests a nickname given to a child.

'He was baby tuckoo' suggests the narrator is a baby.

Inability to pronounce 'r' and 's' sounds correctly suggests a child learning to speak.

The reference to wetting the bed suggests a young child.

'When they were grown up' suggests that the narrator is not yet grown up.

The sentences in the passage are either very long, linked by a string of conjunctions, or very short. The contrast and the jerkiness that result again suggest a child's way of speaking.

Adults, including mother and father, are described only in the most immediate sensory terms (father's beard, mother's smell), and not in terms of personality or character.

The concern with age ('They were older than his father . . .') suggests a child coming to terms with the concept of age, and some people being older than others.

The sudden changes in subject (a song, wetting the bed; hair brushes) and thought association (one thought leading on to another without a logical link, as when the smell of urine links in with the smell of the boy's mother) again suggest a child.

The use of song suggests a child.

A comprehensive commentary on this passage will, however, include more than the above. The first danger is that the student will not recognise the most obvious feature of the passage (one student in an actual examination wrote down in a tone of utter condemnation that the author of this passage was an idiot because he wrote no better than a child!); the second is that once recognised the analysis is not taken any further. For example, the link between the smell of urine and the smell of a mother is comic, as the insult to mothers is clearly unintentional. The sudden changes of subject are quite amusing in a general sense, and not merely in connection with this one passage. The author also suggests with some intensity the uncertainty and strangeness of a child's world, its inability to understand *why* anything happens, its clinging on to particular certainties ('He was baby tuckoo' and 'That was his song'), and its capacity to notice what happens without making any judgement on it. Thus events and people are recorded in the passage, but hardly commented on. The child does not have the knowledge, maturity, or detachment to make comments; it can only experience whatever surrounds him. Something of the terror that the world can hold for a child is suggested by the final refrain 'Pull out his eyes,/Apologize', and is there possibly even to suggest how guilt is programmed into a child from a young age.

If the question seems to invite such comment, a passage such as this is a good opportunity to talk or write about narrative technique. Simple as it is, it could be argued that the language of the passage is too complex for a young child, the vocabulary ('oilsheet', 'queer') too mature. The passage could be seen as an extreme of first-person narrative, or as using some form of the STREAM OF CONSCIOUSNESS (see 'Literary Terms' above) technique. Certainly the limitations of the passage coincide with the limitations of its narrator. The passage is extremely vivid, demands attention, and paints an effective picture of the world seen through the eyes of a child; given that this is what the passage intends to achieve one cannot expect it to present an overall view.

One law of reading the novel (and other forms of literature) is to assume right from the start that anything odd, unusual, or out of the ordinary has a reason for its existence: it is the student's job to find that reason. If a reason cannot be found after long and exhaustive effort, then perhaps what is there in the passage is simply inexplicable; but it is safer to assume that everything has an explanation. Another law is not to take a passage always at face value; it is quite easy, for example, to be fooled by the disguise of IRONY (see pp. 27–8), as in the following passage from *Tom Jones* by Henry Fielding:

He now lived, for the most part, retired in the country, with one sister, for whom he had a very tender affection. This lady was now somewhat past the age of thirty, an aera at which, in the opinion of the malicious, the title of old maid may with no impropriety be assumed. She was of that species of women whom you commend rather for good qualities than beauty, and who are generally called, by their own sex, very good sort of women – as good a sort of woman, madam, as you would wish to know. Indeed, she was so far from regretting want of beauty, that she never mentioned that perfection, if it can be called one, without contempt; and would often thank God she was not as handsome as Miss Such-a-one, whom perhaps beauty had led into errors which she might have otherwise avoided. Miss Bridget Allworthy (for that was the name of this lady) very rightly conceived the charms of person in a woman to be no better than snares for herself, as well as for others; and yet so discreet was she in her conduct, that her prudence was as much on the guard as if she had all the snares to apprehend which were ever laid for her whole sex. Indeed, I have observed, though it may seem unaccountable to the reader, that this guard of prudence, like the trained bands, is always readiest to go on duty where there is the least danger. It often basely and cowardly deserts those paragons for whom the men are all wishing, sighing, dying, and spreading every net in their power; and constantly attends at the heels of that higher order of women for whom the other sex have a more distant and awful respect, and whom (from despair, I suppose, of success) they never venture to attack.

This passage does no more than paint a picture of a certain lady, in guarded terms of praise. Closer examination reveals a cutting irony in almost every line.

> This lady was now somewhat past the age of thirty, an aera at which, in the opinion of the malicious, the title of old maid may with no impropriety be assumed.

At first sight this says that the lady in question is a little over thirty. The key phrase is 'somewhat past the age of thirty', the word 'somewhat' being particularly influential in shaping the reader's response. The fact that care has been taken to qualify the statement that she is over thirty warns the reader and makes him suspicious, adding to the number of years awarded to the lady. The author then states two things: malicious people call such women old maids, and there is nothing wrong or improper in the term. By stating that only malicious people would call her an old maid the author is neatly avoiding calling her one himself, but at the same time planting firmly in the reader's mind the idea that she is an old maid. By telling the reader that there is nothing improper in the term, he alerts the reader to the idea that there *might* be something improper in the term. The outcome of all this is a firm message that the lady is considerably older than thirty, and perhaps lies about her age to conceal it, and that she is a true old maid, or a woman ignored by men. This may be what is implied by the passage, whilst the author has apparently taken great pains to imply nothing of the sort, a fact which adds to the humour of the passage.

Fielding then states that the lady was known for good qualities rather than beauty – outwardly a harmless statement, but one which could easily be taken as stating that she is ugly. The repetition of the phrase 'good woman', and its rendering in semi-colloquial speech, also makes this phrase somewhat suspicious, as though it is of doubtful truth and so has to be repeated if anyone is to believe it. When the lady goes on to condemn beauty in others, it is clear that she is envious of those who have the beauty she cannot claim. The author tells us that she condemned beauty in an apparently neutral tone, but the ironic interpretation given to earlier lines warns the reader to interpret these lines as well in an ironic manner.

At this point Fielding tells us the woman's name, which has so far been withheld. He carries on his pretence of innocence by stating that Miss Bridget Allworthy takes every possible defensive action against seduction, despite the fact that she seems to be in little real danger. The comment on life which follows ('prudence . . . is always readiest to go on duty where there is the least danger') is again apparently innocent, a mere observation on one of the oddities of life, yet it condemns the woman by revealing her hypocrisy and jealousy of those who are in danger of seduction. The author completes the irony by commenting that prudence seems to desert those most in danger when they most need it, but that men do not attempt to seduce women like Miss Allworthy 'from despair, I suppose, of success'. By this time it is quite clear why men do not approach women such as her: they are far too ugly and unattractive to be worth bothering about.

The danger for the author in a passage such as this is that the reader will take what he says at face value. Fielding avoids this by a number of techniques. The woman herself is of a type familiar to most people: neglected by men, bitter, self-righteous, sour, unattractive. All these features are suggested by the phrase 'old maid', and once Fielding can forge a link between the woman and the phrase 'old maid' the damage to her reputation is half-way towards being done – no matter how much he hedges round the phrase with qualifications. Then he qualifies everything he says, as with her age being *somewhat* past thirty. He also makes points by what he does not state. He states she is called a very good sort of woman by her own sex, implying that the opposite sex have a very different view of her. Fielding adopts a tone of bland innocence in his comments, seemingly unable to see the real meaning behind what he is stating, and that meaning is left to the reader to unravel. All the information necessary for the reader to form a hostile picture of Miss Allworthy is there in the passage; the skill of the irony lies in the reader's being allowed to draw the conclusions from it himself, and not have the author spell out to him what he should be thinking. This process of finding out for himself is attractive for the reader. His perception of the gap between what appears to be stated and what is actually stated is also comic, an added bonus for the author. Fielding can claim to have written a straightforward description of an admirable sort of woman, with a few comments on certain ironies of human behaviour; the effect is of a straight condemnation of a wholly hypocritical and unattractive woman.

An equally useful weapon in a novelist's armoury is description. This extract from *Bleak House* by Charles Dickens shows a master of description at work.

While Esther sleeps, and while Esther wakes, it is still wet weather down at the place in Lincolnshire. The rain is ever falling, drip, drip, drip, by day and night, upon the broad flagged terrace-pavement, The Ghost's Walk. The weather is so very bad down in Lincolnshire, that the liveliest imagination can scarcely apprehend its ever being fine again. Not that there is any superabundant life of imagination on the spot, for Sir Leicester is not here (and, truly, even if he were, would not do much for it in that particular), but is in Paris, with my Lady; and solitude, with dusky wings, sits brooding upon Chesney Wold.

There may be some motions of fancy among the lower animals at Chesney Wold. The horses in the stables – the long stables in a barren, red-brick court-yard, where there is a great bell in a turret, and a clock with a large face, which the pigeons who live near it, and who love to perch upon its shoulders, seem to be always consulting – *they* may contemplate some mental pictures of fine weather on occasions, and may be better artists at them than the grooms. The old roan, so famous for cross-country work, turning his large eyeball to the grated window near his rack, may remember the fresh leaves that glisten there at other times, and the scents that stream in, and may have a fine run with the hounds, while the human helper, clearing out the next stall, never stirs beyond his pitchfork and birch-broom. The grey, whose place is opposite the door, and who, with an impatient rattle of his halter, pricks his ears and turns his head so wistfully when it is opened, and to whom the opener says, 'Woa grey, then, steady! Noabody wants you today!' may know it quite as well as the man. The whole seemingly monotonous and uncompanionable half-dozen, stabled together, may pass the long wet hours, when the door is shut, in livelier communication than is held in the servants' hall, or at the Dedlock Arms; – or may even beguile the time by improving (perhaps corrupting) the pony in the loose-box in the corner.

So the mastiff, dozing in his kennel, in the court-yard, with his large head on his paws, may think of the hot sunshine, when the shadows of the stable-building tire his patience out by changing, and leave him, at one time of the day, no broader refuge than the shadow of his own house, where he sits on end, panting and growling short, and very much wanting something to worry, besides himself and his chain. So, now, half-waking and all-winking, he may recall the house full of company, the coach-houses full of vehicles, the stables full of horses, and the out-buildings full of attendants upon horses, until he is undecided about the present, and comes forth to see how it is. Then, with that impatient shake of himself, he may growl in the spirit, 'Rain, rain, rain! Nothing but rain – and no family here!' as he goes in again, and lies down with a gloomy yawn.

So with the dogs in the kennel-buildings across the park, who have their restless fits, and whose doleful voices, when the wind has been very obstinate, have even made it known in the house itself: upstairs, downstairs, and in my lady's chamber. They may hunt the whole countryside, while the raindrops are pattering round their inactivity. So the rabbits with their self-betraying tails, frisking in and out of holes at roots of trees, may be lively with ideas of the breezy days when their ears are blown about, or of those seasons of interest when there are sweet young plants to gnaw. The turkey in the poultry-yard, always troubled with a class-grievance (probably Christmas), may be reminiscent of that summer morning wrongfully taken from him, when he got into the lane among the felled trees, where there was a barn and barley. The discontented goose, who stoops to pass under the old gateway, twenty feet high, may gabble out, if we only knew it, a waddling preference for weather when the gateway casts its shadow on the ground.

Be this as it may, there is not much fancy otherwise stirring at Chesney Wold. If there be a little at any odd moment, it goes, like a little noise in that old echoing place, a long way, and usually leads off to ghosts and mystery.

The opening of the passage – 'While Esther sleeps, and while Esther wakes' – gives the impression of something taking place over a long period of time, spanning at least a night and a day. The repetition of 'drip' and the further reference to something lasting more than a day ('by day and night') concentrate the description on the twin concepts of rain and wetness, and something which has continued and is continuing for a long period of time. The absence of the presumed owners of the house gives a feeling of emptiness, aided by the words 'solitude', 'dusky' (with its hint of 'dusty'), and 'brooding'. The author takes pains to emphasise the absence of 'imagination', perhaps because it suggests liveliness – the one feature absent from the house.

The mention of 'imagination' in the first paragraph is carried through into the remainder of the passage, the difference being that the term now used is 'fancy'. Both terms imply something other than bare fact, a certain liveliness of mind and spirit, but 'fancy' perhaps has a more playful feeling to it, more gaiety and spirit. In any event, the author chooses to use the animals in or around the house to convey his description of it at this particular time. This is seemingly rather strange. The author clearly wishes to present a description of a lifeless house almost inundated with rain and dreary weather, and he might be expected therefore to describe long empty halls, the noise and feel of the rain, and keep any hint of life out of his description. In the text, however, he does almost the exact opposite. The house itself is hardly mentioned, the description concentrates on the only things (the animals) that have any life in them at all, and even then describes largely what they felt like or might feel like at more cheerful times. The author wonders if the 'old roan' remembers summer, if the mastiff remembers the 'hot summer', the goose the time when the hot sun cast a shadow from the gateway.

This apparently contradictory method of describing a sodden house and countryside has a cumulative effect. There are continual reminders throughout the passage of the weather and emptiness of the house. The 'human helper' is suggested as being sunk in apathy. The statement that the 'seemingly monotonous' stable might hold more life than the local inn or the servant's hall in effect suggests that all three are dead and silent. The author is only speculating that the animals may have stimulating thoughts. The mastiff is imagined as saying 'Rain, rain, rain!'; the following paragraph has 'while the raindrops are pattering round their inactivity', combining wetness and inaction in one phrase. The reader is never allowed to lose sight of the prevailing conditions.

The reader knows that the glimpses of summer or a full house given in the passage are imaginary concepts in the minds of animals; as such, they lose a little of the force and power they might have had if they had been seen working in a human mind. In effect the reader knows from the start that the idea of the animals imagining anything in this way is fanciful, and thus increases the fictitious element in what is said. The scenes summoned up of hot summer days and bustling activity are therefore made to seem unreal, and their presence serves to emphasise the bleakness and isolation that start off the passage. The description is oblique: it does not describe the issue in hand, but something else very different from it, and in so doing heightens the reader's awareness of what the original issue is. The fact that animals are imagined as being provoked into yearning for better days carries with it a feeling that the present must be truly dreadful.

Another of Dickens's techniques is the selection of the conditions of the animals. The horses are locked in a stable; the mastiff is chained to his kennel; the dogs are confined to their kennels; the turkey is cooped up in the poultry yard; the goose 'waddles' and 'stoops', suggesting almost an old and crippled fat man. Everywhere the animals are confined, hemmed in by the rain and the isolation, afloat in a sea of solitude, almost in hibernation. The author could have chosen to describe buildings or the countryside in the rain; instead he chooses animals with life in them, but shows this life at a low ebb, run-down and constrained; the description suggests something so dispirited as to drain all but the barest flicker of animation from living things.

There is 'fancy' in the passage, an almost playful wandering in and out of stable and kennel and field and poultry yard, as if the author delights in the freedom he has given himself to go where and when he pleases. Tiredness is suggested a number of times, with the mastiff 'dozing', and giving a 'gloomy yawn'; and discontent is also suggested with the 'doleful' sound of the dogs, the turkey with a 'class-grievance', and the 'discontented goose'. However much the description might seem to stray from the two concepts of rain and dreary emptiness, these two concepts underpin the whole passage, and are its most consistent element. The description is visual, but not exclusively so; sound, and smell are used, as are descriptions of various abstract moods. The sheer variety of the techniques used can serve to hide the extent to which the passage concentrates on the atmosphere suggested in the opening section and in the final paragraph.

Part 6

Revision

KNOWING YOUR TEXTS and understanding them is one thing; bringing all the information you need to boiling point at exactly the right time for an examination is another. How you revise will depend on the number and nature of the books you have studied; the type of questions you are likely to be asked; the length of the examination; and a number of personal factors which will vary from candidate to candidate.

There are three basic elements from which all students revise, and a number of minor ones.

The text

Naturally enough, this is the crucial factor, and the one you have to start with. As with all aspects of revision, it is not just *what* you do with the text, but *when* you do it that matters. For an 'A' level, an effective revision programme will start at least three months before the first examination; for an 'O' level, six weeks is a minimum period. There is no point in starting too early, the risk being that you have learnt it all two or three weeks before the examination and then go stale and start forgetting what you have learnt. Start too late and you are liable to miss things out, or see everything as being equally important.

You should have a good, modern text, almost always the edition recommended by the examining board (this is not possible sometimes; boards do have a habit of recommending texts that are out of print). If you have used a cheap copy of the text for most of your course, or used the one that happened to be lying on a bookshelf at home, at least buy or obtain a regulation edition for your revision. Your text should have printed notes in it written by the editor, translating difficult words or passages, or making critical comments. Sometimes the editor's notes are at the bottom of each page; sometimes they are on the opposite page; sometimes they are hidden away at the back. You should also write your own notes in your copy of the text, notes that you have made during lessons, from what the teacher has said.

The first thing to do when revising your text is to read through it carefully once, word by word. As you do so:

(a) Make sure you understand at least the meaning of everything you read. If you cannot understand it, and there is nothing that helps in the notes, put a line by the side of the the word or passage, and get help from a teacher.

(b) Try to memorise your own comments at the same time as you are reading the text. This is much easier if your own notes are written directly above or by the side of the passage to which they refer.

(c) Scrutinise the editor's printed notes as you read the text, and underline or write in those which seem particularly relevant, even if they are on the opposite page. Writing out a summary of the note or underlining concentrates your mind in a manner that reading on its own will never do.

All this takes a long time, and it can be very depressing when you realise how long it has taken, how many more books you still have to do, and how much you still do not know. It is at this point that the basic motto of revision ('Don't panic!') comes into force. Your first detailed reading through the text will take a long time, and at the end of it all you still will not know it all. The point is that the first effort of this nature is the hardest – later readings will take progressively less and less time. When you first start learning it takes a long time, and you will probably only remember what you have learnt for a few days. The next time it takes less time, and you remember for longer, and so on, until you are learning more and more in less and less time.

After this first marathon, your text will be very messy and cluttered with scribblings, but it means that as you read a line you are killing three birds with one stone: you are learning the text, your own comments, and those of the editor, all at the same time. Equally, it can be a very helpful aid to buy the cheapest paperback edition of your text, and check how much you have remembered by glancing at the unmarked pages of this occasionally. There is something very comforting about using your own text with all your notes and underlining marked in; it can be a rude but very helpful shock to read an unmarked text (which is how you will see the text in an examination if a passage is reprinted), and realise how much you have not learnt. Also, going back to an unmarked text does allow you to think up new responses to the book, which you should always be able to make. It is very easy to assume that what you wrote originally on a passage is all there is to say about it, and this is very rarely true.

Always plan to read through a text three times before an examination, remembering that it will take less and less time with each reading. On the second and third readings, try to get a feel for the book or play *as a whole.* Lessons very often chop books up into little pieces so that the student can write well on individual scenes or poems, but has little feel for the overall structure of a novel or play, or the general lines along which a poet writes.

Notes

Not all the notes you will have made will be in the text. It is very likely that at least some will be lecture notes, taken down either in class from a teacher, or during your readings of any critical studies. There is no point in learning these first. After all, they are simply devices for ordering and arranging what is to be found in the actual text, and so it makes no sense at all to start with these; start with the text.

A major cause of nervous collapse in examination students is their first careful look at their notes. Sometimes there simply are none; the student has dreamed his time away in lessons, failed to read any books on his subject, and has a completely blank file. Again, do not panic; if you start early enough, you can make up lost ground. If you really have nothing at all from which to revise, borrow another student's notes and take what you can from them. If there are books you have failed to read and know you ought to have read, simply get out, find the books, and make brief notes. The urgency of the operation, done at the last minute, actually need not be a disadvantage. It forces you to be economical and not simply rewrite the book you are reading, and often gives much more concise, economical notes to use in your revision.

Anyone who is reading a book such as this Handbook is likely to be a little more organised and conscientious than the student in the above predicament. This does not mean an absence of problems. An average set of notes, looked at two or three months before an examination, will be likely to produce a number of horrors. Notes on different books, and even on different subjects, may be crammed in with each other in a totally disorganised manner. The notes are very probably in bits and pieces: half a side here, three lines there, and so on, depending on how interesting you found the lesson, whether or not you had other things on your mind, and so on. Your first revision task, therefore, is to get organised. All notes on a given book should be put into one section, split off from all others. If they really are in bits and pieces, sit down and rewrite them, so one topic follows on from another, and you are not faced with blank pages at every turn. Sort out what you have missed, and what is absent from the file. You are bound to have missed lessons, not read a certain book you were told to read, or otherwise have left gaps. When you first read your notes draw up a list of areas and topics you have not covered satisfactorily and start filling the gaps immediately. Here again, leaving yourself enough time is vital. Probably the single most useful book for anyone studying Shakespearian tragedy (at least the one students are told most often to read) is A. C. Bradley's *Shakespearian Tragedy*. If you have not read it during your course, you can be sure a lot of other students are in a similar position. Come the examination time, there is great pressure on the school or college library, and woe betide any poor student who leaves his copy lying around. If you start early enough, the books are still available from libraries, and you can read them in relative peace and quiet, without a hungry horde of students breathing down your neck.

First time through, read all your notes. Learn as much as you can. Plug any gaps that there are in your reading or noting. On the second reading, try to summarise what you have written in the briefest possible form. Third time round, set yourself the task of producing a list of basic points contained in your notes, trying to squeeze it all on one or two sides of paper. Concentrating it in this manner forces you to think about it, and gives you something simple and straightforward to read through as the last thing you do before the examination.

Essays

Essays are very useful to revise from; they are also very dangerous. Under normal circumstances, every book you study will have a number of recognised topics to it, of the sort that an examiner is likely to be interested in, and the essays you have written in class will reflect these standard areas of interest. If you simply learn an essay, you are learning information assembled with the aim of answering one particular question. Disaster threatens if in an examination you are tempted to reproduce the essay you wrote before when the examination question is not quite the same. A typical example is an essay that students of *Hamlet* often answer: 'Is Hamlet mad?'. If you learn this essay off by heart and then see a question on your examination paper that reads 'Why does Hamlet go mad?' there is a strong urge to let your examination answer slide gently into the answer you wrote before – yet the two questions are not the same, and demand a different approach.

However, the information in essays can be immensely useful. The trick is not to learn it as a block, but to remember the various pieces of information in your essays as something movable and portable, which can be turned to answer a number of possible essay titles.

You should work through your essays and write down a list of all the mistakes you have made. You will probably find there is a surprising degree of consistency in these. Just as every human being has different, unique fingerprints, so each student has his or her own list of common mistakes. Spellings are an obvious one, and an easy one to remedy. 'Arguement' for 'argument', 'tradgedy' for 'tragedy' – there are numerous minor spelling areas which tend to crop up time and time again in each student's particular style of writing. Your job when revising is to make a list of these and other persistent mistakes, and learn the correct way once and for all. What you should do is to make a list of the things you do *not* do well: spellings, planning, paragraph organisation, use of slang, failure to write correct introductions and conclusions, failure to answer the title, and failure to produce enough quotations, or to write them down without explaining them fully, these are probably the most common. Revision is the time to tackle these recurrent problems (sometimes so minor that they have never seemed worth a major effort before), and make sure they are remedied well before the examination. There is no point in revision if all you are going to learn is your mistakes; and a surprising amount of marks can be saved by tidying up minor punctuation and grammatical mistakes.

General points

There are a number of other devices or approaches that can make revision both more bearable and more effective.

Audio and visual aids

If you can get hold of a record or cassette of the text you are studying, so much the better. Listen to it, following it in the text as you do so. It is often quicker than reading it to yourself, it has variety, and it can give you a new and different insight into the text: the actor reading the poem or the actors acting the play often see lines very differently from your own private image, and even if you do not agree with their interpretation, it is still something new to liven up a text with which you probably are becoming rather too familiar. It is usually not a good idea to listen more than twice to a tape or record, largely because you reach the stage where you cease to be able to think of the work being acted or delivered any other way. With a video, or even a film – if you are lucky enough to be able to arrange either – tread very carefully. If it is a play you are watching, you can very easily start thinking of it only in terms of the scenery and actors of the one particular production, thus giving yourself a very limited vision. You can hear a play, poem, or novel two or even three times without necessarily losing sight of other ways in which it might be performed, but when you see it and hear it, particularly if it is the only production you do see, once is sometimes enough to limit your vision.

Varying the diet

When you are familiar with a text, you can probably sit down and read through a play or book of poems in one sitting; a novel might well take longer. There are advantages, referred to earlier, in doing this, mainly for the way it allows you to develop a 'feel' for the book or work as a whole. However, when you are undertaking the first, detailed read-through for revision, you should learn to monitor your own concentration. If it is a difficult book, or one you really do not enjoy, do not punish yourself by reading it all at one go; break it up into smaller sections, so you never spend so long with it that you really begin to get bored and start to feel ill at the mere sight of the text. Be imaginative in dividing the book up into sections. If it is a novel that was published in weekly or monthly instalments, read it in the original instalments first time round, thus breaking it up and also giving yourself an idea of how the novel appeared to its original readership. Work out where the interval should be in a play, and read it in two or three sections. If it is a collection or book of poems, divide the poems up into roughly equal blocks of poems linked by style, or themes. Mix your revision; do one hour's work on a book you do not like, and bribe yourself with the promise that you will spend the second hour on a book you enjoy more. Remember that hard revision is to a certain extent a battle between yourself and your own mind, and it is up to you to devise ways of avoiding an excess of boredom while still doing what you have to do.

Timing yourself

Literature examinations rarely last for less than one and a half hours; three hours is a maximum. Remember that when you come to sit the examination, you will be required to maintain full concentration for whatever the length of the examination happens to be. Very often your class work will have trained you to concentrate for whatever the length of a standard lesson is in your school, usually not less than half an hour, rarely more than one hour. If you are used to concentrating for one hour, you will find a three-hour examination very testing, so plan for this in your revision. Try working in three-hour sessions, if that is how long your examination lasts, so that it is not a shock for you when the examination comes round.

A possible programme

There is no such thing as a standard programme of revision. Your revision programme has to be planned, not only to ensure that you cover the necessary ground, but also to ensure that you play to your own particular strengths and weaknesses. What follows is an outline only; by the time you come to revise, you should know quite a lot about how you work, and so vary the programme to fit your own requirements.

(1) Take the full syllabus for your examination, and break it down into its separate, constituent parts, writing these down on a sheet of paper. For example, a traditional literature 'A' level syllabus might be broken down as follows:

(a) Shakespeare, *Hamlet**
(b) Shakespeare, *Twelfth Night**
(c) Chaucer, *The Knight's Tale**
(d) Dickens, *Bleak House**
(e) Poems by John Donne
(f) Jane Austen, *Pride and Prejudice*
(g) George Bernard Shaw, *Major Barbara*
(h) Seamus Heaney, *Death of a Naturalist*

Here the division is simple; the syllabus breaks down into eight texts, those marked with an asterisk requiring detailed textual knowledge, those without the asterisk needing less detailed knowledge. For other examinations, there might be a section of 'Comment and Appreciation', a section on general literary topics, or even a section with language work or knowledge of current affairs in it.

When you have divided up the syllabus like this, what you have is a list of all the areas that you will have to revise in order to be fully prepared for the examination, topic by topic. As a rough guide, you will need to go through each topic thoroughly three times before the examination.

(2) Work out which topics you know the most about, and which you know the least about; which you enjoy most, which you least like. Plan your revision accordingly. Start your revision with the topic or book you know least about, finish with the one you have already done the most work on. Alternate topics or books you enjoy with ones you do not like, so that there is always something to look forward to.

(3) When you have been through a topic fully – text, notes, and essays – put a tick by it on your list. Your aim is that all the topics should have three ticks by them by the time of the examination. Without this simple check, you might well find that you have been through the topics you enjoy several times, and only looked briefly at those you find more difficult or less attractive. This can prove a disaster: an examination does not discriminate between what you like and what you do not like, and the candidate with a broad knowledge of his syllabus is the only one who can go into the examination room with a clear conscience and full confidence.

(4) Time yourself as you revise one topic or book fully. Work out roughly from this how long it will take you to complete the full syllabus; this estimate will not be entirely accurate, but it will serve as a base from which to start. Then, on another sheet of paper, write a timetable for one week at a time, with a blank box for the periods when you will be free to revise. For the average student in a day school, still required to attend some lessons but with others given free for revision, a timetable might look like this (see over):

	Mon.	Tues.	Wed.	Thurs.	Fri.	Sat.	Sun.
Early morning							
9 a.m.–12.30 p.m.							
2 p.m.–4 p.m.							
4 p.m.–6 p.m.							
7 p.m.–10 p.m.							
10 p.m.–late night							

The student has put a line through the times when he or she knows revision is not possible; either there are lessons then, or other commitments which cannot be overlooked.

(5) Decide which are the best times for you to work. Some people work best early in the morning; others do not really begin to function at all before mid-day. Whichever time suits you best, you will not last the day if you try to work both in the early morning and late at night. Designate your time on the basis of (a) when you work best (b) when you could work if you had to (c) times at which you can only work if it is a desperate emergency.

(6) Plan each week's work and write in on the timetable what you plan to do and when. Use the times first in category (a), and try to leave the (c) times blank for emergencies, as for instance when a topic takes three times as long to revise as you thought it would, or when you realise that there is a whole topic you left out of your original list. Vary the programme as suggested in section (2) above.

Plans, of course, look marvellous, and are completely useless unless the student actually sticks to them. It is not the plan that matters so much as actually doing the work. The advantage of a plan is that it lets you decide what to do and when, the whole thing being aimed at your particular strengths and weaknesses. You write down on the plan what you think you will do, but it will be very rare for a week to go by without you failing to do at least one session: at four o'clock you are suddenly asked to a marvellous party that evening, when you had planned to read through the complete text of *Hamlet*; or a teacher calls you in at short notice for a lesson; or you suddenly find the football team of which you are a member has arranged an extra fixture, and the coach has forgotten to tell you. The advantage of a plan is that if you cannot do what you intended to do, you are at least aware of the fact, and you can use one of your 'reserve' times to make up lost ground. Without a plan, it is all too easy to forget that you never did actually go through this or that topic, only to find when you see your examination paper, that this is exactly what you are being asked to write on.

Never be over-optimistic about how much revision you will be able to do. Take one day of the week completely off. Never plan to work *all* day: nine hours a day is the maximum the average student can cope with, and even that – if you are really concentrating – can only be sustained for a few weeks.

(7) Keep a record of how many hours' work a day you have done. It is all too easy to do a massive ten-hour stint on one day, and then do nothing for the next three or four days, whereas an altogether more relaxed three hours a day for five days would have covered much more ground at much less cost.

(8) Remember that it is not the number of hours you spend in front of your books that produces good results so much as what you do in those hours. It is much better to work for one hour and really concentrate than work for four hours with your mind on something else.

(9) When you are first revising a text, make a list of quotations for use in the actual examination. Do not try to restrict this overmuch, just write down separately all the lines you think might be useful when it comes to answering your questions in the examination. Then, when you have been through all your notes and essays as well, go back and choose not more than forty lines to learn for the examination. Try to choose short extracts, one for each of the major points that you know now are in the book.

(10) On your final revision, try to make a brief summary of your notes and essays, if possible on one side of paper.

Knowing the books

Reading through a text and notes can become very tedious after a while, so much so that the student feels he is not learning anything new and is merely going over and over familiar ground. Here are some things that can be done with texts in order to make revision more stimulating and therefore interesting, as well as more useful.

Drama
1. Summarise the content of each scene in a play, as briefly as possible.
2. Identify and write out the six or so most important speeches in the play.

3. Identify the six most crucial episodes or scenes in the play, and write a short critical passage on each.
4. Go through the play concentrating on one major character.
5. Do the same for a minor character.

Poetry
1. Write out and learn by heart about one hundred lines, either whole poems or extracts.
2. Read aloud – and ideally record on tape – any number of poems, the more the better.
3. Choose three poems and write on them, showing either how they are generally typical of the author, or how they illustrate certain particular qualities of the author.
4. Identify a poet's major themes, and group his poems according to them.
5. Take five poems at random and list their particular elements of style and construction.

Prose
1. Examine the start and the end of the novel; describe the extent to which the start of a novel matches what follows, and how effectively the ending brings to a conclusion all the features in it.
2. Make short summaries of all the chapters; or list the characters and then note the points in the text where they appear.
3. Identify five crucial episodes in the novel, and write short critical notes on them.
4. Take an unmarked copy of the novel, and re-read it simply as a novel (but have a piece of paper handy to write down any thoughts which spring to mind as you read through).
5. Attempt to reconstruct any incident from the novel without consulting the text, and then see how much your version differs from the original.

By giving you something specific to do whilst reading through or revising, the above suggestions should ensure that you do not waste time when reading through, and that you focus on the text in a concentrated manner.

Part 7

Select reading list

READING LISTS ARE COMMON FEATURES in any English Literature course, and yet they are all too frequently ignored. This chapter does not present a reading list in the sense of a list of books which the student is expected to read or have read. It is not a comprehensive list of the hundred or so 'best' works in English literature. It contains very little in the way of critical works on individual authors. What it does set out to do however, is to give publishing details of the books mentioned at the end of the various groups in the 'History and Reading List' sections, so that these books can be traced, ordered, or bought if necessary. In addition it lists a small number of other texts and critical works for which there was no room in the 'History of Reading Lists' sections.

Editions suggested in this list are not always the best-known, the cheapest, or the most readily available. They do, however, generally represent the best value for money, and the highest standards of accuracy. Many of the books, if not all, were originally published in hardback editions, and are now available in paperback. Publishing history is not given here, merely the publisher, place, and date of publication of the most recent edition. Editions have been chosen primarily because they have a proven record of success with students, through format, price, content, or presentation.

Even a list as long as this barely scratches the surface. Remember you will gain more marks from having read the text thoroughly than you will ever gain from having read what someone else has written about that text.

Anthologies

Anthologies (collections of work by different authors) do exist for prose and drama, but are often less successful than poetry anthologies, largely because the length of the average play or novel means that only short works can be included, or longer ones have to be savagely cut. Thus only poetry anthologies are included below. They can be used to gain a general background knowledge of a period or author, or to save purchasing a large number of separate texts. Care needs to be exercised when buying an anthology; it is rare for an anthology to contain all an author's significant work, and something is usually left out. On the other hand, some examining boards list anthologies as set texts, in recognition of the fact that a broad knowledge of a period or group can be as useful as a narrow, detailed knowledge of one author.

ALVAREZ, A. (ED.): *The New Poetry*, Penguin Books, Harmondsworth, 1966.

GARDNER, BRIAN (ED.): *Up the Line to Death: War Poets 1914–18*, Magnum Books (Methuen), London, 1976.

GARDNER, HELEN (ED.): *The Metaphysical Poets*, Penguin Books, Harmondsworth, 1972.

The Mersey Sound, Penguin Modern Poets No.10 (Adrian Henri, Roger McGough, Brian Patten), Penguin Books, Harmondsworth, 1967.

WRIGHT, DAVID (ED.): *The Penguin Book of English Romantic Verse*, Penguin Books, Harmondsworth, 1968.

Texts

AUDEN, W. H.: *Selected Poems*, Faber & Faber, London, 1968.

AUSTEN, JANE: *Pride and Prejudice*, Penguin Books, Harmondsworth, 1972.

BECKETT, SAMUEL: *Waiting for Godot*, Faber & Faber, London, 1965.

BLAKE, WILLIAM: *The Essential Blake*, ed. A. Kazin, Chatto & Windus, London, 1968.

BRONTË, CHARLOTTE: *Jane Eyre*, Penguin Books, Harmondsworth, 1966.

BRONTË, EMILY: *Wuthering Heights*, Penguin Books, Harmondsworth, 1965.

BROWNING, ROBERT: *Selected Poems*, ed. James Reeves, Heinemann, London, 1959.

BYRON: *Poetical Works*, Oxford University Press, London, 1945.

CHAUCER, GEOFFREY: *The Canterbury Tales*, Everyman's Library, Dent, London, 1958.

COLERIDGE, SAMUEL TAYLOR: *Selected Poems*, Heinemann, London, 1959.

CONGREVE, WILLIAM: *The Way of the World*, ed. Brian Gibbons, New Mermaid Series, Ernest Benn, London, 1971; ed. A. Norman Jeffares, Edward Arnold, London, 1966. (The latter edition includes Congreve's novel *Incognita*.)

CONRAD, JOSEPH: *Heart of Darkness/Typhoon*, Pan Books, London, 1976.

DEFOE, DANIEL: *Moll Flanders*, Everyman's Library, Dent, London, 1972.

DICKENS, CHARLES: *Oliver Twist*, Penguin Books, Harmondsworth, 1966.

———: *Great Expectations*, Penguin Books, Harmondsworth, 1965.

———: *Bleak House*, Penguin Books, Harmondsworth, 1971.

DONNE, JOHN: *Poems*, ed. James Reeves, Heinemann, London, 1974.

DRYDEN, JOHN: *Selected Poems*, ed. Roger Sharrock, Heinemann, London, 1963.

———: *All for Love*, ed. Arthur Sale, University Tutorial Press, London, 1957.

ELIOT, GEORGE: *Middlemarch*, Penguin Books, Harmondsworth, 1970.

ELIOT, T. S.: *Murder in the Cathedral*, Faber & Faber, London, 1968.

————: *The Waste Land and Other Poems*, Faber & Faber, London, 1972.

Everyman, in *Medieval Miracle Plays*, ed. A. C. Cawley, Dent, London, 1974.

FARQUHAR, GEORGE: *The Beaux' Stratagem*, New Mermaid Series, Ernest Benn, London 1976.

FIELDING, HENRY: *Tom Jones*, Penguin Books, Harmondsworth, 1966.

FORSTER, E.M.: *Howard's End*, Penguin Books, Harmondsworth, 1975.

GOLDSMITH, OLIVER: *The Plays and Poems of Oliver Goldsmith*, Everyman's Library, Dent, London, 1910.

GREENE, GRAHAM: *Brighton Rock*, Penguin Books, Harmondsworth, 1975.

GUNN, THOM and HUGHES, TED: *Selected Poems*, Faber & Faber, London, 1963.

HARDY, THOMAS: *Far From the Madding Crowd*, Pan Books, London, 1967.

————: *The New Wessex Selection of Thomas Hardy's Poetry*, Macmillan, London, 1976.

————: *Tess of the D'Urbervilles*, Macmillan, London, 1974.

HEANEY, SEAMUS: *Death of a Naturalist*, Faber & Faber, London, 1969.

HINES, BARRY: *Kes*, Penguin Books, Harmondsworth, 1965.

JAMES, HENRY: *Portrait of a Lady*, Penguin Books, Harmondsworth, 1969.

JONSON, BEN: *The Alchemist*, ed. Douglas Brown, New Mermaid Series, Ernest Benn, London, 1972.

JOYCE, JAMES: *A Portrait of the Artist as a Young Man*, Penguin Books, Harmondsworth, 1960.

————: *Ulysses*, Penguin Books, Harmondsworth, 1969.

KEATS, JOHN: *The Poetical Works of John Keats*, World's Classics Series No.7, Oxford University Press, London, 1928.

KYD, THOMAS: *The Spanish Tragedy*, ed. P. Edwards, Revels Plays, Manchester University Press, Manchester, 1972.

LARKIN, PHILIP: *The Whitsun Weddings*, Faber & Faber, London, 1964.

LAWRENCE, D. H.: *The Rainbow*, Penguin Books, Harmondsworth, 1949.

MARLOWE, CHRISTOPHER: *Doctor Faustus*, ed. Roma Gill, New Mermaid Series, Ernest Benn, London, 1965.

MARVELL, ANDREW: *Andrew Marvell: Some Poems*, ed. James Winny, Hutchinson, London, 1962.

MILTON, JOHN: *Paradise Lost Books I & II*, ed. P. Brockbank and C. A. Patrides, Macmillan, London, 1972.

————: *Samson Agonistes*, in *The English Poems of John Milton*, ed. H. C. Beeching, World's Classics Series No.182, Oxford University Press, London, 1946.

ORWELL, GEORGE: *Animal Farm*, Penguin Books, Harmondsworth, 1951.

OSBORNE, JOHN: *Look Back in Anger*, Faber & Faber, London, 1960.

OTWAY, THOMAS: *Venice Preserv'd*, ed. M. M. Kelsall, Regent's Restoration Drama Series, Arnold, London, 1969.

PINTER, HAROLD: *The Birthday Party*, Eyre Methuen, London, 1975.

POPE, ALEXANDER: *The Poems of Alexander Pope*, ed. John Butt, Methuen University Paperbacks, Methuen, London, 1968.

SASSOON, SIEGFRIED: *Selected Poems*, Faber & Faber, London, 1968.

SHAKESPEARE, WILLIAM: There are so many editions of Shakespeare's plays and poems that a simple list is neither possible nor desirable, particularly as new editions appear regularly. For the *Complete Works* the text by Professor Peter Alexander first published by Collins in its modern edition in 1951 is the standard authority. 'A' level students usually turn to either the 'New Swan' edition published by Longman, the 'Arden' texts published by Methuen, or occasionally the 'Signet' edition published by the New American Library. A cheap and reliable paperback edition is that published by Penguin Books, and the Cambridge Shakespeare, published by the Cambridge University Press, is equally good.

SHAW, BERNARD: *Saint Joan*, Penguin Books, Harmondsworth, 1946.

SHELLEY, PERCY BYSSHE: *Selected Poems*, ed. John Holloway, Heinemann, London, 1960.

SHERIDAN, R. B.: *The School for Scandal*, ed. C. J. L. Price, Oxford University Press, London, 1971; also ed. A. Norman Jeffares, Macmillan, London, 1967.

SOPHOCLES: *Oedipus Rex* (*Oedipus the King*), in *Theban Plays*, trans. E. F. Watling, Penguin Books, Harmondsworth, 1947.

STOPPARD, TOM: *Rosencrantz and Guildenstern Are Dead*, Faber & Faber, London, 1968.

SWIFT, JONATHAN: *Gulliver's Travels*, Penguin Books, Harmondsworth, 1967.

TENNYSON, ALFRED LORD: *Selected Poems*, ed. Stephen Gwynn, World's Classics Series No.51, Oxford University Press, London, 1950.

THACKERAY, WILLIAM: *Vanity Fair*, Penguin Books, Harmondsworth, 1968.

TOURNEUR, CYRIL: *The Revenger's Tragedy*, ed. Brian Gibbons, New Mermaid Series, Ernest Benn, London, 1971.

VANBRUGH, JOHN: *The Relapse*, ed. Bernard Harris, New Mermaid Series, Ernest Benn, London, 1971.

WAUGH, EVELYN: *Decline and Fall*, Penguin Books, Harmondsworth, 1937.

WEBSTER, JOHN: *The Duchess of Malfi*, ed. Clive Hart, Oliver & Boyd, Edinburgh, 1972.

WELLS, H. G.: *The History of Mr Polly*, Pan Books, London, 1963.

WILDE, OSCAR: *The Importance of Being Earnest*, Eyre Methuen, London, 1966.
WORDSWORTH, WILLIAM: *Selected Poetry and Prose*, ed. W. M. Merchant, Rupert Hart-Davis, London, 1967.
YEATS, W. B.: *Selected Poems*, ed. A. Norman Jeffares, Pan Books, London, 1965.

Criticism

General criticism
BATESON, F. W.: *A Guide to English Literature*, Longman, London, 1967. This is a good guide to further reading.
BECKSON, KARL, and GANZ, A.: *A Reader's Guide to Literary Terms*, Thames & Hudson, London, 1961.
COOMBES, H.: *Literature and Criticism*, Penguin Books, Harmondsworth, 1963. An excellent introduction to literary criticism.
IFOR-EVANS, B.: *A Short History of English Literature*, Penguin Books, Harmondsworth, 1976. This is the revised edition of this classic work, still arguably the best short history of English literature.

In addition to the above there are at least two standard companions or guides to English literature. *The Oxford Companion to English Literature* (edited and compiled by Sir Paul Harvey, Oxford University Press, London, 1967) is a dictionary of authors, titles, characters and other useful information. *The Penguin Companion to Literature Volume I: British and Commonwealth* (edited by David Daiches, Penguin Books, Harmondsworth, 1971) deals solely with authors, listed alphabetically, and gives a concise listing of all their works, and a brief critical commentary both on individual works and the standing of the author as a whole. On a slightly larger scale there is the well-established *Pelican Guide to English Literature* published by Penguin Books in seven volumes ranging from Chaucer to the present day; the *Sphere History of Literature in the English Language*, again in several volumes, and published by Sphere Books, London; and the *Macmillan History of Literature*, in twelve or nine volumes, published by Macmillan, London, 1982.

Criticism: drama
BRADLEY, A. C.: *Shakespearian Tragedy*, Macmillan, London, 1974.
BRADBROOK, M. C.: *Themes and Conventions of Jacobean Drama*, Cambridge University Press, Cambridge, 1973.
CHARLTON, H. B.: *Shakespearian Comedy*, Methuen, London, 1966.
CUNNINGHAM, J.: *Restoration Drama*, Literature in Perspective Series, Evans, London, 1966.
DOVER WILSON, J.: *The Fortunes of Falstaff*, Cambridge University Press, Cambridge, 1964.

154 · Select reading list

ELLIS-FERMOR, UNA: *The Jacobean Drama*, Methuen, London, 1965.
ESSLIN, MARTIN: *Theatre of the Absurd*, Penguin Books, Harmondsworth, 1980.
GRANVILLE-BARKER, HARLEY: *Prefaces to Shakespeare*, Volumes 1–5, Batsford, London, 1970.
HARTNOLL, PHYLLIS: *A Concise History of the Theatre*, Thames & Hudson, London, 1968.
LEECH, CLIFFORD: *Tragedy*, Critical Idiom Series, Methuen, London, 1969.
RUSSELL TAYLOR, JOHN: *The Penguin Dictionary of the Theatre*, Penguin Books, Harmondsworth, 1974.
THOMPSON, CARGILL: *An Introduction to Fifty British Plays 1660–1900*, Pan Literature Guides, Pan Books, London, 1979.
TILLYARD, E. M. W.: *Shakespeare's Problem Plays*, Penguin Books, Harmondsworth, 1965.
————: *The Elizabethan World Picture*, Penguin Books, Harmondsworth, 1972.

Criticism: poetry
BENNETT, JOAN: *Five Metaphysical Poets*, Cambridge University Press, Cambridge, 1964.
BERGONZI, BERNARD: *Heroes' Twilight: A Study of the Literature of the Great War*, Constable, London, 1965.
FUSSELL, PAUL: *The Great War and Modern Memory*, Oxford University Press, 1977.
GROSE, M. W.: *Chaucer*, Literature in Perspective Series, Evans, London, 1967.
HUNTER, J.: *Metaphysical Poets*, Literature in Perspective Series, Evans, London, 1965.
HUSSEY, M., SPEARING, A. and WINNY, J.: *An Introduction to Chaucer*, Cambridge University Press, Cambridge, 1968.
————: *Chaucer's World: A Pictorial Companion*, Cambridge University Press, Cambridge, 1967.
PRESS, JOHN: *A Map of Modern English Verse*, Oxford University Press, London, 1969.
REEVES, J.: *Understanding Poetry*, Pan Books, London, 1967.
RICKS, C.: *Milton's Grand Style*, Oxford University Press, London, 1963.
SCHMIDT, MICHAEL: *An Introduction to Fifty British Poets, 1300–1900*, Pan Literature Guides, Pan Books, London, 1979.
SCOTT, A. F.: *Close Readings*, Heinemann, London, 1968.
STALLWORTHY, JON: *Wilfred Owen*, Oxford University Press and Chatto & Windus, London, 1974.
STEAD, C. K.: *The New Poetic: Yeats to Eliot*, Penguin Books, Harmondsworth, 1967.

SUTHERLAND, JAMES: *A Preface to Eighteenth-Century Poetry*, Oxford University Press, London, 1963.

THWAITE, ANTHONY: *Poetry Today, 1960–1973*, Longman, London, 1973.

WALDOCK, A. J. A.: *Paradise Lost and Its Critics*, Cambridge University Press, Cambridge, 1966.

Criticism: The novel

FORSTER, E. M.: *Aspects of the Novel*, Penguin Books, Harmondsworth, 1976.

KETTLE, ARNOLD: *An Introduction to the English Novel* (two volumes), Hutchinson University Library, London, 1967.

PHELPS, GILBERT: *An Introduction to Fifty British Novels, 1600–1900*, Pan Literature Guides, Pan Books, London, 1979.

POPE-HENNESSY, UNA: *Charles Dickens*, Penguin Books, Harmondsworth, 1970.

WATT, IAN: *The Rise of the Novel*, Penguin Books (Pelican), Harmondsworth, 1963.

WILSON, ANGUS: *The World of Charles Dickens*, Secker & Warburg, London, 1970.

Index

162 · Index

YORK HANDBOOKS

Further titles

STUDYING CHAUCER
ELISABETH BREWER

The study of set books is always more interesting, rewarding and successful when the student is able to 'read around' the subject. But students faced with such a task will know the difficulties confronting them as they try to tackle work outside the prescribed texts. This Handbook is designed to help students to overcome this problem by offering guidance to the whole of Chaucer's output. An introduction to Chaucer's life and times is followed by a brief description and analysis of all his works, identifying the major issues and themes. The author also discusses contemporary literary conventions, and Chaucer's use of language.

Elisabeth Brewer is Lecturer in English at Homerton College of Education, Cambridge.

STUDYING SHAKESPEARE
MARTIN STEPHEN AND PHILIP FRANKS

Similar in aims to *Studying Chaucer*, this Handbook presents an account of Shakespeare's life and work in general, followed by a brief analysis of each of the plays by Shakespeare which might usefully be studied as background reading for a set book. Philip Franks then throws a different light on the study of Shakespeare by giving an account of his experiences of Shakespeare in performance from his perspective as a professional actor and member of the Royal Shakespeare Company.

Martin Stephen is Second Master at Sedbergh School; Philip Franks is a professional actor.

PREPARING FOR EXAMINATIONS IN ENGLISH LITERATURE
NEIL McEWAN

This Handbook is specifically designed for all students of English literature who are approaching those final months of revision before an examination. The purpose of the volume is to provide a sound background to the study of set books and topics, placing them within the context and perspective of their particular genres. The author also draws on his wide experience as a teacher of English both in England and abroad to give advice on approaches to study, essay writing, and examination techniques.

Neil McEwan is Lecturer in English at the University of Qatar.

ENGLISH USAGE
COLIN G. HEY

The correct and precise use of English is one of the keys to success in examinations. 'Compared with' or 'compared to'? 'Imply' or 'infer'? 'Principal' or 'principle'? Such questions may be traditional areas of doubt in daily conversation, but examiners do not take such a lenient view. The author deals with many of these tricky problems individually, but also shows that confidence in writing correct English comes with an understanding of how the English language has evolved, and of the logic behind grammatical structure, spelling and punctuation. The Handbook concludes with some samples of English prose which demonstrate the effectiveness and appeal of good English usage.

Colin G. Hey is a former Inspector of Schools in Birmingham and Chief Inspector of English with the Sudanese Ministry of Education.

A DICTIONARY OF LITERARY TERMS
MARTIN GRAY

Over one thousand literary terms are dealt with in this Handbook, with definitions, explanations and examples. Entries range from general topics (comedy, epic, metre, romanticism) to more specific terms (acrostic, enjambment, malapropism, onomatopoeia) and specialist technical language (catalexis, deconstruction, *haiku*, paeon). In other words, this single, concise volume should meet the needs of anyone searching for clarification of terms found in the study of literature.

Martin Gray is Lecturer in English at the University of Stirling.

READING THE SCREEN
An Introduction to Film Studies
JOHN IZOD

The world of cinema and television has become the focus of more an more literary work, and film studies is a fast-growing subject in schools and universities. The intention of this Handbook is to introduce the film viewer to the range of techniques available to the film maker for the transmission of his message, and to analyse the effects achieved by these techniques. This Handbook is geared in particular to students beginning a course in film studies – but it also has a great deal to offer any member of the film-going public who wishes to have a deeper understanding of the medium.

John Izod is Lecturer in Charge of Film and Media Studies at the University of Stirling.

The first 200 titles

The author of this Handbook

MARTIN STEPHEN was educated at Uppingham School. He received a Combined Honours degree in English and History from the University of Leeds, and a PH.D. from the University of Sheffield. He has taught in a wide range of schools and institutions including a number of years as a teacher of English and a housemaster at Haileybury College. He has made several appearances on radio and television as a musician, and held contracts as a professional artist. He is at present Second Master of Sedbergh School. He has written six titles in the York Notes series, various Theatre-in-Education works, and is working on a critical biography of poets of the First World War. He is also the author of the York Handbook, *Studying Shakespeare.*